THE BEDFORD SERIES IN HISTORY AND CULTURE

Black Americans in the Revolutionary Era

A Brief History with Documents

Related Titles in
THE BEDFORD SERIES IN HISTORY AND CULTURE
Advisory Editors: Lynn Hunt, *University of California, Los Angeles*
David W. Blight, *Yale University*
Bonnie G. Smith, *Rutgers University*
Natalie Zemon Davis, *Princeton University*
Ernest R. May, *Harvard University*

THE BEDFORD SERIES IN HISTORY AND CULTURE

Black Americans in the Revolutionary Era

A Brief History with Documents

Woody Holton

University of Richmond

BEDFORD/ST. MARTIN'S   Boston   ◆   New York

Dedicated to Peter H. Wood, teacher and friend

For Bedford/St. Martin's

Publisher for History: Mary V. Dougherty
Director of Development for History: Jane Knetzger
Executive Editor: William J. Lombardo
Senior Editor: Heidi L. Hood
Developmental Editor: Ann Hofstra Grogg
Editorial Assistants: Katherine Flynn, Jennifer Jovin
Production Associate: Samuel Jones
Executive Marketing Manager: Jenna Bookin Barry
Text Design: Claire Seng-Niemoeller
Project Management: Books By Design, Inc.
Index: Books By Design, Inc.
Cover Design: Joy Lin
Cover Art: John Singleton Copley, *Head of a Negro*, 1777/1778, Founders Society
  Purchase. Gibbs-Williams Fund. Photograph © 1986 Detroit Institute of the Arts.
  Copley was living in London when he painted his sensitive study of a black man. The
  identity of the man is not known, but the strongest possibilities are that he was born
  in the Americas of African parents or that he was born in Africa and transported to
  the Americas. It also remains a mystery whether he was transported to London
  willingly or unwillingly.
Composition: TexTech International
Printing and Binding: RR Donnelley & Sons Company

President: Joan E. Feinberg
Editorial Director: Denise B. Wydra
Director of Marketing: Karen R. Soeltz
Director of Editing, Design, and Production: Marcia Cohen
Assistant Director of Editing, Design, and Production: Elise S. Kaiser
Manager, Publishing Services: Emily Berleth

Library of Congress Control Number: 2008934226

For information, write: Bedford/St. Martin's, 75 Arlington Street,
Boston, MA 02116   (617-399-4000)

ISBN-10: 0-312-41359-9
ISBN-13: 978-0-312-41359-0

Acknowledgments

Document 21: SC1/series 45X, Massachusetts Archives Collection, v. 186: p. 134–136a,
Paul Cuffee and others, Petition against taxation, February 10, 1780.

Document 26: SC1/series 230, House Unpassed Legislation, 1787 #2358, Prince Hall
and others, Petition for return to Africa, January 4, 1787.

Distributed outside North America by PALGRAVE MACMILLAN.

Foreword

The Bedford Series in History and Culture is designed so that readers can study the past as historians do.

The historian's first task is finding the evidence. Documents, letters, memoirs, interviews, pictures, movies, novels, or poems can provide facts and clues. Then the historian questions and compares the sources. There is more to do than in a courtroom, for hearsay evidence is welcome, and the historian is usually looking for answers beyond act and motive. Different views of an event may be as important as a single verdict. How a story is told may yield as much information as what it says.

Along the way the historian seeks help from other historians and perhaps from specialists in other disciplines. Finally, it is time to write, to decide on an interpretation and how to arrange the evidence for readers.

Each book in this series contains an important historical document or group of documents, each document a witness from the past and open to interpretation in different ways. The documents are combined with some element of historical narrative—an introduction or a biographical essay, for example—that provides students with an analysis of the primary source material and important background information about the world in which it was produced.

Each book in the series focuses on a specific topic within a specific historical period. Each provides a basis for lively thought and discussion about several aspects of the topic and the historian's role. Each is short enough (and inexpensive enough) to be a reasonable one-week assignment in a college course. Whether as classroom or personal reading, each book in the series provides firsthand experience of the challenge—and fun—of discovering, recreating, and interpreting the past.

Lynn Hunt
David W. Blight
Bonnie G. Smith
Natalie Zemon Davis
Ernest R. May

Preface

For African Americans, the Revolutionary era of 1750–1800 brought monumental gains and devastating losses. Some slaves achieved freedom through petitions to courts or as a reward for service in the Patriot army. Even larger numbers emancipated themselves by fleeing to the British, who then resettled them in Canada and Africa. For those black Americans who remained in the new United States, however, the ideology of the Revolution fell far short of its promise. Almost all of them remained enslaved. The small number who were free found their lives constrained by prejudice and discrimination. The black role in the revolutionary cause was largely forgotten. Only through the recent surge of scholarly interest in African Americans in the founding era is their profound impact on the Patriots' decision for independence and on the course of the war starting to be recognized. *Black Americans in the Revolutionary Era* examines this impact through a fresh look at liberty and freedom from the perspective of a people who experienced the struggle for American independence at both the personal and political levels.

The book opens with a comprehensive introduction that provides background essential for understanding the revolutionary era. It begins by surveying black American life, both slave and free, in the North and the South, on the eve of the Revolution. Then, mirroring the organization of the documents in the second part of the book, it addresses the role of black Americans in the coming of the Revolution, their participation in military service during the war, and their struggles for freedom and dignity in the postwar era.

Black Americans' diverse experiences and influence before, during, and after the Revolution are revealed in the wide assortment of primary sources included in the second part of the book. Alongside the familiar writings of Phillis Wheatley and Benjamin Banneker are the memoirs of lesser known black Americans who fought in the Continental Army, founded churches, launched rebellions, and escaped to the British lines, exchanging military service for freedom in exile. There are also freedom petitions claiming that the principles of the Declaration of Independence applied as much to African Americans as to slaveholding Founding Fathers like Thomas Jefferson and George Washington. The final document is an excerpt from the first book-length history of black participation in the Revolutionary War, published in 1855 by a black abolitionist.

Complementing these documents are primary sources from white Americans that illuminate issues of slavery and freedom. Included are fugitive slave advertisements, an excerpt from a plantation diary, a letter from Patrick Henry musing on slavery's profits and evils, a Christian defense of slavery and a Quaker denunciation of it, and Jefferson's assertion that Africans are intellectually inferior to Europeans. Some documents are visuals—depictions of African Americans in battle, at work, and as remembered by friends. Taken together, the range of materials in this book reflects the breadth of the sources available for African American history.

To enrich students' understanding of the documents, each is preceded by a headnote that establishes its context. Unfamiliar words and out-of-date usages are explained in notes at the bottoms of pages. The book concludes with helpful supplemental material. The detailed chronology will prompt students to reach their own conclusions about causes and effects. The questions for consideration are meant to elicit thought-provoking class discussions and writing assignments. Students will find sufficient evidence in the documents to respond to these questions, but there is no single right answer for any of them. The selected bibliography lists additional primary sources as well as secondary sources, most published in the last ten years.

A NOTE ON THE TEXT

Most of the selections in this book were transcribed directly from the original documents. Spelling has not been modernized and punctuation has not been corrected. Paragraph breaks have been added to enhance readability. In transcriptions from handwritten documents, sentence breaks are added only where the author indisputably intended them.

ACKNOWLEDGMENTS

More than anything else I have written, *Black Americans in the Revolutionary Era* has been a team effort. I am grateful to everyone at Bedford/St. Martin's who made the book possible, especially Patricia Rossi, who signed it; Mary Dougherty, who championed it; Jane Knetzger, who sustained it; and Heidi Hood, Katherine Flynn, and Jennifer Jovin, who saw it to completion. Kylie Horney and Nancy Benjamin provided keen insights at the final stages of the editing process. I especially want to acknowledge Ann Hofstra Grogg, my developmental editor, who contributed so much to the book that she really ought to be listed as a co-author; I have never known anyone who combines good writing and goodwill to the extent that Ann does.

In addition, I wish to acknowledge the help of the following readers of earlier drafts for their insightful comments: Jennifer Baszile, Yale University; Robert E. Desrochers Jr., Emory University; Ellen Eslinger, DePaul University; Thomas J. Humphrey, Cleveland State University; Allan Kulikoff, University of Georgia; Maxine N. Lurie, Seton Hall University; Leonard J. Sadosky, Iowa State University; Dorothy Salem, Cuyahoga Community College; Matthew C. Whitaker, Arizona State University; and Calvin White Jr., University of Arkansas. I also want to thank the teachers who first piqued my interest in African and African American history: Paul M. Gaston, Joseph C. Miller, and the late Armistead Robinson at the University of Virginia; and William H. Chafe, Janet J. Ewald, Barry Gaspar, Julius S. Scott, and Peter H. Wood (who also served as a reviewer and to whom this book is dedicated) at Duke University.

Woody Holton

Contents

Illustrations

PART ONE

Introduction: African American Freedom and American Independence

One of the remarkable ironies of the American Revolution is that nearly all of the Founding Fathers—George Washington, Thomas Jefferson, and the rest—did everything they could to prevent the era's greatest act of liberation. This was the decision of thousands of enslaved African Americans—including slaves belonging to Washington and Jefferson—to seek freedom. Many African Americans did in fact achieve liberty during the War of Independence, mostly by forming what was in essence an alliance not with the Founding Fathers but with their enemy, the British.

Service in the British army or navy was not the slaves' only route to freedom. Some were liberated in return for fighting on the Patriot side. Others were freed by owners moved by Christian piety or the Revolution's libertarian ideals. If we think of freedom as the most cherished value of the founding era, then we must see it as inspiring not only famous revolutionaries such as Washington and Jefferson but also thousands of their African American contemporaries.

Yet the hard fact was that the vast majority of African Americans remained in slavery after the United States secured its independence with victory over the British at Yorktown in 1781 and peace in 1783. Many, in fact, lived in more difficult conditions than before the war. A Patriot's slave who tried but failed to reach the British lines was sometimes punished by being sold to a sugar plantation in the Caribbean, enduring harsher work routines than in North America and never seeing friends and family again. Those who remained on the mainland endured wartime deprivations and outbreaks of smallpox, typhus, and other diseases, perishing at a higher rate than any group except Native Americans. In short, while some African Americans seized freedom in the midst of the war's disruptions, others suffered even worse than before.

Even as the Revolutionary War had an enormous impact on African Americans, they in turn played a crucial role in influencing the course of the conflict. Black soldiers, spies, and, most of all, guides helped both the Patriots and the British turn defeats into victories. In many engagements, such as the battle of Monmouth, New Jersey, on June 28, 1778, African Americans fought on both sides.[1] But even before the first battles at Lexington and Concord in 1775, slaves recognized that they could use the rift between the colonists and Britain to their advantage. The informal partnership they formed with the British infuriated white colonists, pushing many toward the drastic step of declaring independence.

BLACK AMERICAN LIFE ON THE EVE OF WHITE INDEPENDENCE

The first African Americans arrived in the New World in the early 1500s — a century before Jamestown — as the slaves of Spanish explorers. By 1770, there were nearly a half million African Americans in the thirteen British colonies that would declare independence six years later. The total number of colonists was just over two million, so blacks made up slightly more than one-fifth of the population. In the southern provinces, 40 percent of all settlers were African American.[2] Most worked in agriculture, predominantly on plantations in the colonies bordering the Chesapeake Bay, in the Carolinas, and in Georgia. Before the Revolution, they grew tobacco, rice, indigo, and only a little cotton. Some were house servants, but many others learned and practiced a wide variety of skills. For instance, many black men worked as sailors on merchant ships (Documents 2 and 37).

Whatever their conditions of life and labor, slaves made frequent attempts to escape. Most had little hope of obtaining permanent freedom; they simply wanted to visit family members or to temporarily leave behind the harsh work and the indignities of plantation life, even knowing they would be punished when they returned or were recaptured. When slaves had been gone for extended periods, their owners often published newspaper advertisements offering rewards for their return. These notices provide information not only about the forms of resistance that enslaved Americans chose but also about their daily lives. Like other sources authored by slaveholders, such as diaries, the advertisements must be used with great caution, since they reflect the prejudices of people who held negative attitudes about African Americans. Yet the scarcity of black-authored documents leaves historians with little choice but to try to use white-authored documents to learn what they can about African American life in the era of the American Revolution (Documents 1 and 4).

Although life for most slaves was a constant struggle against the people who claimed to own them, the vast majority managed to make it something more than that. Sometimes with their masters' encouragement, but more often in the face of brutal opposition, they created vibrant religious lives. Before the early eighteenth century, few African Americans converted to their owners' Christian faith. But in a series of revivals that began in the 1730s—known to historians as the Great Awakening—blacks began to convert in large numbers (Document 24). As a result, blacks and whites of the Revolutionary era worshipped together at a much higher rate than they do today. African Americans were especially prominent in the Baptist and Methodist denominations, but they also began to found churches of their own. In Frederick County, Maryland, a black community built a Methodist church in 1766. In the early 1770s, a preacher named David George and his congregation founded a black Baptist church at Silver Bluff, South Carolina (Document 33). Boston King, a South Carolina slave who escaped to the British and later wrote his memoirs, remembered his father leading the family in nightly prayers (Document 34).

Tangible evidence of black religious faith may be found in African Americans' poems and other writings. The first black American to publish a poem was a slave named Jupiter Hammon, whose "Evening Thought" appeared in 1760. In 1773, the Boston slave Phillis Wheatley traveled to London to promote her book *Poems on Various Subjects* (Document 9), the first book ever published by an African American. Both black poets struggled to understand slavery in the light of Christian principles. Undoubtedly their owners as well as their white audiences influenced their work, and their most inward thoughts are difficult to discern. Hammon seemed to accept his enslavement in one poem: "if we are slaves it is by the permission of God." But he also said of white Americans, "I must say that I have hoped that God would open their eyes, when they were so much engaged for liberty, to think of the state of the poor blacks, and to pity us."[3]

Wheatley left an equally ambiguous record. Her poems display Christian devotion but also contempt for racial prejudice. In a published letter to Samson Occom, a Presbyterian minister, she makes her most forthright claims for equality: "in every human Breast, God has implanted a Principle, which we call Love of Freedom; it is impatient of Oppression, and pants for Deliverance" (Document 10).

At the same time that Wheatley was struggling with oppression in the context of Christian belief, religion was motivating a growing number of white Americans to turn against slavery. The Society of Friends, whose members were known as Quakers, opposed slavery and gradually worked toward the position that slaveowners had to leave the society. John Woolman of New Jersey, Anthony Benezet of Pennsylvania, and other Quakers dedicated their lives to the abolition of slavery (Document 5).

BLACK AMERICANS AND THE COMING OF THE AMERICAN REVOLUTION

The relationship between enslaved and free Americans was forever changed by the advent of the American Revolution. The independence movement unfolded in two principal phases. The military conflict started on April 19, 1775, with the battles of Lexington and Concord, and ended in 1783, when Great Britain signed a peace treaty with its former colonists. That was the second phase. Earlier, between the years 1763 and 1775, what can be called the imperial conflict focused on the actions of the British Parliament, which, for the first time, asserted the right to tax the American colonists directly. The Stamp Act, adopted by Parliament in 1765, required that newspaper advertisements, deeds transferring real estate, and other documents—even playing cards—bear a costly stamp, with the proceeds helping to finance the colonial governments and the British troops stationed in North America. The Townshend duties (1767) levied tariffs on several items the colonists imported, from lead and glass to painters' colors and—most ominously—tea. During these years, the British also tried to wipe out colonial smuggling. Merchants were not the only colonists who suffered. Britain's so-called Proclamation of 1763 was an attempt to stop white colonists from provoking Indian wars by encroaching on the natives' land, now generally defined as all of the territory west of the Appalachian Mountains.

In the 1760s and early 1770s, most free American colonists protested Parliament's new requirements but remained loyal to Britain. They tarred and feathered stamp collectors and boycotted British merchandise. In Boston in 1770, when a company of British soldiers fired into a threatening crowd, killing five, the colonists christened the incident the Boston Massacre. In the most famous of all the protests, Bostonians boarded three tea ships on the night of December 16, 1773, and threw their cargoes into the harbor.

Enslaved Americans did not need to learn the value of freedom from their Patriot owners. Yet the Revolution, with its focus on liberty and natural rights, did provide African Americans with a useful language with which to express their long-standing grievances. Slaves were quick to seize this new opportunity. For example, shortly after white colonists paraded through Charleston, South Carolina, in 1765, to protest the Stamp Act, they were startled to learn that a group of black South Carolinians had raised their own cry of "liberty." In the early 1770s, enslaved subjects in the colony of Massachusetts began sending petitions to the provincial assembly and royal governor asking to be freed (Documents 6 and 8). In her published letter to Samson Occom, the Mohegan Indian who had become a Presbyterian missionary, Phillis Wheatley likewise drew heavily on the language of liberty (Document 10).

Enslaved Americans like Wheatley repeatedly pointed out the hypocrisy of those who inveighed against British attempts to impose political slavery upon free colonists while practicing actual slavery themselves. Increasingly, the slaves' message got through. In a 1770 essay, Benjamin Franklin imagined a conversation between an Englishman and a white American. "You Americans make a great Clamour upon every little imaginary Infringement of what you take to be your Liberties," Franklin's Englishman declares, "and yet there are no People upon Earth such Enemies to Liberty, such absolute Tyrants" as the white Americans who held their fellow humans in bondage. Abigail Adams expressed a similar view. "It allways appeard a most iniquitious Scheme," she wrote her husband John while he was attending the First Continental Congress in September 1774, to "fight ourselfs for what we are daily robbing and plundering from those who have as good a right to freedom as we have."[4] Two attorneys at the forefront of the Patriot cause, James Otis of Massachusetts and Patrick Henry of Virginia, also acknowledged that African Americans deserved to share in the rights for which their free neighbors were contending (Documents 3 and 7). On the other side of the Atlantic, Edmund Burke, a pro-American member of Parliament, speculated that the colonists' tendency to "snuff the approach of tyranny in every tainted breeze" was owing to their familiarity with slavery. In fact, the language of colonial protest often used the image of slavery. "Is life so dear, or peace so sweet," Patrick Henry asked in his famous "liberty or death" speech of March 23, 1775, "to be purchased at the price of chains and slavery?" So numerous were these images of slavery that one historian has called chattel slavery "the nightmare of the American Revolutionaries."[5]

As 1775 opened, the majority of the white colonists between New Hampshire and Georgia were angry at British policies regarding taxation, territory, and trade, yet very few wished to declare independence. Most simply wanted to turn back the clock—to restore the relationship between the crown and colonies to what it had been in 1763, before British imperial officials began demanding unprecedented sacrifices from their American colonists. Yet by the end of 1775, most white Americans had begun to express a bold new demand for independence. Why did white Patriots' goals change so radically over the course of a single year? Among the most important factors were the battles of Lexington and Concord and the colonists' discovery that the British government had hired Hessian mercenaries for service in America. It was becoming increasingly clear that British officials were fully prepared to spill American blood.

In the South, another factor helped convince white Americans to demand more than the restoration of the old crown-colony relationship. White southerners were furious at the British government for collaborating with their slaves. The Continental Congress referred to this collaboration in the Declaration of Independence, asserting that King George III had "excited domestic insurrections amongst us."

Congress wished to convey the impression that the British had fomented uprisings by slaves who might otherwise have remained passive. A careful review of the chronology of the relationship between the British and black Americans, however, shows that it was often the slaves who incited the British. African American initiatives began in the fall of 1774, when very few white Americans were angry enough at Britain to favor independence. In September, Abigail Adams learned that a group of Massachusetts slaves planned to write the state's embattled Loyalist governor, Thomas Gage, "telling him they would fight for him provided he would arm them and engage to liberate them if conquerd." Slaves in Virginia made similar plans. "In one of our Counties lately," James Madison reported in November, "a few of those unhappy wretches met together & chose a leader who was to conduct them when the English Troops should arrive." Enslaved workers in other colonies also gathered to discuss how to take advantage of the imperial conflict. A group of slaves who rebelled in St. Andrew's Parish, Georgia, in December 1774, killing four whites before they were captured and executed, may also have been inspired by the widening rift between white Patriots and Loyalists.[6]

During the third week of April 1775, more rumors of slave plots poured into Williamsburg, the capital of Virginia, than during any previous week in Virginia history. At the end of that week, the royal governor, Lord Dunmore, decided to remove Virginia's gunpowder supply from the magazine in the center of Williamsburg and secure it on a British warship. Dunmore, a loyal supporter of the imperial government, was probably just trying to keep the gunpowder out of Patriot hands. But white Virginians believed Dunmore had deliberately removed the gunpowder amid the swirl of slave insurrection rumors in order to abandon them to the fury of their slaves. In his *History of Virginia*, Edmund Randolph, who had lived in Williamsburg in April 1775, said the governor "designed, by disarming the people, to weaken the means of opposing an insurrection of the slaves ... for a protection against whom in part the magazine was at first built."[7]

Governor Dunmore seemed to confirm these suspicions when he responded to a Patriot ultimatum demanding the return of the gunpowder by proclaiming that if Patriots harmed him or any other British official, he "would declare freedom to the slaves and reduce the city of Wmsburg to ashes." A provincial official told the governor he had lost "the Confidence of the People not so much for having taken the Powder as for the declaration he made of raising and freeing the Slaves." A group of blacks who had heard about Dunmore's threat presented themselves at the Governor's Palace, offering to defend him if he would free them. Dunmore revealed that for the moment, at least, his threat had been an empty one. He sent the slaves away and threatened to whip them if they returned.[8]

Slaves in other colonies also went on the offensive. In Ulster County, New York, during the winter of 1774–1775, two slaves who were allegedly involved in a conspiracy were overheard discussing how to obtain more lead shot (bullets) and gunpowder. In early July 1775, when white North Carolinians discovered a widespread plot among their slaves, they also learned that the slave rebels had been promised British aid. According to militia colonel John Simpson, the plan was for blacks to start a rebellion on the night of July 8. They were to kill their owners and then move westward toward the backcountry, where "they were to be received with open arms by a number of Persons there appointed and armed by Government for their Protection."[9]

Many enslaved Americans carried the rumors about British aid for black insurrection one step further: they believed that the whole purpose of the expected British invasion of the south was to liberate them. In the spring of 1775, an enslaved South Carolinian alleged that Thomas Jeremiah, a free black harbor pilot, had told slaves "the War was come to help the poor Negroes."[10] Jeremiah was executed, becoming the first southerner of any race to die in the Revolutionary War. Farther south in St. Bartholomew parish at about the same time, a black preacher named George told gatherings of slaves "That the Young King, meaning our Present One, came up with the Book, & was about to alter the World, & set the Negroes Free." George was executed.[11] The widespread belief among many black southerners that their freedom was Britain's chief war aim was detected by some whites. John Drayton, a white South Carolinian, wrote many years after the Revolution that the slaves' conviction that the London government meant to instigate an insurrection was "the more alarming; because, it was already known, they entertained ideas, that the present contest was for obliging us to give them their liberty."[12]

Although Governor Dunmore had not immediately acted on his April 1775 threat to free the slaves, black Virginians kept trying to reach him (Document 11). Eventually, the governor began to welcome the slaves whose skills he needed most, and prominent among them was Joseph Harris of Hampton, Virginia. Officially, Harris was the property of another Hamptonian, Henry King, whom he served as a pilot on Chesapeake Bay. Harris, it was said, was "well acquainted with many creeks on the *Eastern* Shore, at *York*, *James* River, and *Nansemond*, and many others." All in all, he was "a very useful person." So in July 1775, when Harris managed to reach the small British fleet operating in Virginia, he was immediately put to work as a pilot. On September 5, 1775, a hurricane drove the ship he was piloting, the *Liberty*, ashore near Hampton. Harris managed to rescue himself and his captain by paddling a borrowed canoe across the mile-wide James River to the safety of the British fleet. Angry Patriots demanded that Dunmore return Harris to his owner, and Dunmore's refusal helped bring on the October 27 battle of Hampton—the first Revolutionary War battle fought south of New England. Harris played an important role in that encounter as well. Moments before his boat fell into enemy hands, he plunged into the icy river and swam with his captain to the British fleet. That made twice in two months that Harris had escorted his commanding officer to safety.[13]

Other black Virginians who joined Governor Dunmore also proved themselves in battle. On November 14 at Kemp's Landing south of Norfolk, Dunmore's outnumbered force, made up largely of former slaves, defeated three hundred members of the Patriot militia of Princess Anne County, killed several militiamen, and set the rest to flight. The Patriot commander, Joseph Hutchings, was captured by two of his own former slaves.[14] Kemp's Landing settled any doubts Dunmore may have had about the usefulness of fugitive slaves as British soldiers. The very next day, the governor issued a proclamation establishing martial law, calling upon free colonists to enlist in his ranks, and also promising freedom to any Patriot's slave who would fight for the king (Document 12).

In the following months, perhaps a thousand slaves left their owners and joined Dunmore. Enlisted in an "Ethiopian Regiment" and wearing inscriptions that proclaimed "Liberty to Slaves," former slaves soon made up the major part of the Loyalist troops.[15] One immediate benefit to Dunmore's black recruits was newfound confidence. A man whom whites called Yellow Peter escaped one day in 1775 or 1776 and was later seen "in Governor Dunmore's regiment with a musket on his back and a sword by his side." He had changed his name to *Captain Peter*.[16]

While Dunmore addressed his proclamation to rebels' slaves "able and willing to bear Arms," and so apparently only to men, more than half the people who joined him were women and children. One of the women listed in the "morning returns of Lord Dunmore's *black banditti*," published in a Patriot newspaper, was Mary Halstead. Sometime in the winter of 1775–1776, she grabbed her three-year-old daughter Phillis and made a mad dash for the British lines. The two got in safely and spent the war serving the British army in New York City.[17]

Dunmore's emancipation proclamation also had an enormous impact on whites, whose fears of slave insurrection led many to demand independence. No other British agent made such an explicit offer to the slaves before July 4, 1776, but as more and more imperial officials quietly welcomed the black men and women who made it to their lines, whites began to see Dunmore's proclamation not as an isolated offer but as general British policy. Archibald Cary of Chesterfield County, Virginia, observed that Dunmore's collaboration with the slaves had driven many whites into the arms of the Patriots. "Men of all ranks resent the pointing a dagger to their Throats, thru the hands of their Slaves," he said. Edward Rutledge of South Carolina expected that the "proclamation issued by Lord Dunmore" would tend "more effectually to work an eternal separation between Great Britain and the Colonies,—than any other expedient, which could possibly have been thought of." In North Carolina in June 1776, patriot James Iredell said that when royal officials encouraged enslaved Americans "to cut our throats," they "added spurs to our Patriotism."[18]

Thomas Jefferson's denunciation of Dunmore's proclamation was one of the most vivid and emotion-laden of the specific charges in his draft of the Declaration of Independence (Document 13). It did not survive the editing process. Indeed, Jefferson's fellow members of the Second Continental Congress removed every direct reference to slaves, simply denouncing King George III for having "excited domestic insurrections amongst us." The congressmen, embarrassed about rebelling against British tyranny while continuing to hold slaves, had deliberately transformed one of the most dramatic of Jefferson's charges into the vaguest grievance on the list.

BLACK AMERICANS IN MILITARY SERVICE

Even as some African Americans were forming alliances with British officials, further alienating them from the free colonists, others were becoming Patriots. Numerous slaves fought at Lexington, Concord, and Bunker Hill in 1775. Prince Estabrook, a slave and minuteman, was among those wounded at the battle of Lexington. At Bunker Hill, a black man, Peter Salem, killed Major John Pitcairn, who had commanded the British forces at Lexington and Concord (Document 16).

On June 17, 1775, the very day several black Patriots fought at the battle of Bunker Hill, Congress commissioned a southern slaveholder as the commander in chief of the newly formed Continental Army. When George Washington arrived at Cambridge to take up his duties, he was appalled at what appeared to him to be the total disorder of the New England soldiers. He set about reforming the army, and one of his reforms—adopted by his Council of War on October 8, 1775— was to remove slaves and even free blacks from the Continental Army.

This ban on black military service lasted less than two months. In December, after Washington learned of Governor Dunmore's proclamation, he grew concerned that free blacks thrown out of work by the war's disruption of the economy would enlist in the British army. Moreover, Washington had labor problems of his own. An extensive Continental Army recruitment campaign at the end of 1775 failed to produce the expected number of volunteers. So Washington addressed both concerns by allowing free blacks (but not slaves) to reenlist in the Continental Army.

Yet even Washington's change of heart did not clear the way for free blacks to enlist, because most of the colonies—and later states—initially prohibited them from doing so. Eventually, however, the states north of Virginia had so much trouble filling their quotas that they felt compelled to allow both free blacks and slaves to sign up. Maryland was the only state with a large slave population that allowed bondmen to enlist. Hundreds did. Their service was the primary reason the free segment of Maryland's black population soared to 20 percent by 1810—the highest of any state that had not abolished slavery. Almost all slaves who signed up were freed; in general, the state government paid the slave's owner his value instead of paying the black soldier an enlistment bounty. In New York, the legislature offered slaveowners land bounties if they would provide slaves to the New York line of the Continental Army. The slaveowner got the land, the army got a soldier, and the slave—if he survived the war—got his freedom.

Virginia and North Carolina permitted the enlistment of free blacks but not slaves. Only South Carolina and Georgia barred all blacks from their militias and Continental lines. (In 1779, when Congress advised South Carolina leaders to start enlisting slaves, they were so appalled at the suggestion that they considered taking South Carolina out of the war.) In all but these two southernmost states, the hard realities of recruitment had overridden the policy pronouncements not only of state legislators and congressmen but also of the commander in chief. And even in the southern states, slaves were sometimes enlisted in defiance of the law.[19]

Blacks volunteered for the army at a considerably higher rate than most other Americans. For instance, in Concord, Massachusetts, blacks made up less than 2 percent of the population but 8 percent of the town's contribution to the Continental Army. In Virginia, more than half the free black men of military age joined up.[20] By the winter of 1777–1778—the hard, cold winter at Valley Forge—one thousand of the eleven thousand soldiers in the Continental Army were black.

Massachusetts and Rhode Island formed military units that consisted entirely or mostly of African Americans. The muster rolls of an all-black Connecticut company show that many of the enlistees had taken proud new surnames such as Freeman, Freedom, and Liberty. Yet most blacks who enlisted in the Continental Army served in racially integrated units. Many earned distinction in battle (Documents 18 and 19). They participated in Washington's famous crossing of the Delaware River on Christmas night 1776 to attack Hessian troops at Trenton, New Jersey, and in the October 1777 defeat of General John Burgoyne at Saratoga, New York—the victory that persuaded the French government to enter the war on the American side. In July 1779, a former slave named Pompey Lamb played an indispensible role in the capture of an invaluable prize: Stony Point, a British fort guarding the Hudson River. The British garrison was unable to detect the American troops' approach because Lamb had guided them to the fort along a secret route. Lamb, who had previously delivered fruit to the fort, diverted the British sentry so American soldiers could seize and gag him. When the war moved south later in 1779, black Patriots moved with it, and several figured in the final victory at Yorktown, Virginia, in October 1781.[21]

Not all African American contributions to the war effort were made on the battlefield. One black Patriot, John Peterson, was captured and confined on a British prison ship (imperial commanders found it cheaper to crowd their American prisoners onto old hulks than to build jails for them). He escaped by clambering down the anchor chain. Soon afterward, he helped prevent the escape of John André, the British spy who had arranged Benedict Arnold's treason. André was supposed to meet a British barge, but as the barge approached the bank of the Hudson River, Peterson and Moses Sherwood opened fire, preventing the rescue party from landing. André was later captured and executed.[22]

Many blacks served the Patriots as sailors, some working on naval vessels and others on privateers—government-sanctioned pirate ships. Prominent among them was James Forten, who served on the *Royal Louis*. On its second cruise, the ship was captured, and Forten and other sailors were sent to the notorious British prison ship the *New Jersey*. After the war, Forten started a sailmaking business and became one of the first black Americans to amass a fortune. Later Forten and his family devoted time, talent, and thousands of dollars to the anti-slavery cause (Document 38).

Even more African Americans fought on the British side. Hundreds of enslaved Virginians fought under Governor Dunmore in 1775 and 1776. Dunmore had to evacuate the state on August 7, 1776, but African American involvement in the British war effort had just begun. During the next two years, while British generals focused on the northern states, British navy captains frequently raided southern plantations, seizing food and other valuables while liberating slaves. Among those who escaped slavery during these raids was Thomas Peters, a millwright from Wilmington, North Carolina. By 1776, when he liberated himself, Peters had already seen more of the world than most of his neighbors ever would. He had been born about 1738 in Yoruba country (in modern-day Nigeria). In 1760, he was kidnapped and sold to the captain of a French slave ship, who carried him to Louisiana. He tried to escape three times, with the result that he was whipped, branded, and shackled. Sometime before 1770, Peters was sold to William Campbell, a Scot who had settled in Wilmington on the Cape Fear River. In March 1776, a twenty-ship British fleet commanded by Sir Henry Clinton sailed up the Cape Fear, and Peters somehow managed to get aboard. Becoming a corporal in a military unit called the Black Guides and Pioneers, he spent the winter of 1777–1778 with the British army that occupied Philadelphia. That winter, common British soldiers like Peters had nearly as much trouble keeping warm as the American soldiers quartered at nearby Valley Forge. Peters served throughout the war and was wounded twice. In 1783, when African Americans who had fought in the British army and their families were evacuated from New York City, Peters was among them.[23]

Most African Americans in the British army served alongside white soldiers (often in support units such as the Wagon Master General's Department), but Thomas Peters's unit, the Black Guides and Pioneers, was staffed entirely by African Americans; only the officers were white. The number of slaves who enlisted in the imperial army swelled late in the war when the major action shifted south. Indeed, two black men helped the British to their first major victory of the southern campaign. General Archibald Campbell's fleet arrived off Savannah, Georgia, in December 1778 and was helped over the sandbar by a black pilot.[24] Then Campbell's soldiers laid siege to the city. When American troops sallied out from Savannah to try to break the siege, Campbell planned to meet them head-on, but a slave named Quamino Dolly persuaded the general to allow him to lead part of the British army along a little-known path around the American lines. Having out-flanked the Americans, Campbell was able to capture Savannah on December 29, 1778.[25]

Less than a year later, on October 9, 1779, a joint French-American army tried to recapture Savannah. Among the blacks who risked reenslavement should the city be retaken were the Baptist minister

David George and his wife, who served as a laundress for General Henry Clinton, now commander in chief of all British forces in North America (Document 33). Some 620 African Americans—many of whom had helped the British capture Savannah—now aided in its defense.[26] Black guides led British reinforcements into town along paths unknown to the French and Continental besiegers, and the siege was broken.

On the Patriot side, some 545 black soldiers had been recruited by the French on the Caribbean island of Saint-Domingue (Haiti). They played a role in the struggle for Savannah, covering the unsuccessful French besiegers' retreat and preventing it from turning into a rout. Among them was twelve-year-old Henri Christophe, a servant and shoe-shiner for the French officers in the Haitian regiment. He would later become king of independent Haiti.

After successfully defending Savannah, the British army headed north. On June 30, 1779, General Clinton issued a proclamation similar to Governor Dunmore's, offering freedom to any Patriot's slave who could make it to the British lines. Some tens of thousands responded. Among them were thirty people who had been owned by Thomas Jefferson. They joined British raiding parties that briefly occupied several of his plantations in 1781.

In addition to serving the king as regular soldiers (Document 15), some African Americans fought in pro-British guerrilla bands. These small groups of fighters have received little attention from military historians, but they engaged in some of the bloodiest fighting of the war (Document 14). There were guerrilla bands on the Patriot side as well, though many fewer blacks joined them. African Americans also served effectively, at their great peril, as spies for both sides (Document 17). Another risky task frequently undertaken by African Americans was carrying messages across hostile territory, as Boston King did shortly after joining with the British (Document 34). Other slaves managed to escape their owners without enlisting in any military unit; they simply took advantage of the wartime confusion to disappear.

One reason some fugitive slaves declined to put themselves under the protection of King George was that the British often deceived them. More than once, the British tested white Patriots' loyalties by promising to return their slaves if they swore allegiance to the king. Several British officers took fugitive slaves who had fought loyally under them to the Caribbean sugar islands and sold them into servitude more brutal than that they experienced on the mainland.

Moreover, thousands of the African Americans who made it to the British lines soon died from the infectious diseases that circulated freely in the army camps. The most lethal of these was smallpox, which infected (but did not kill) two of the fugitives who later wrote their memoirs, David George (Document 33) and Boston King (Document 34). At least one British general was not above using blacks who had come down with smallpox to spread the infection to whites. "About 700 Negroes are come down the River in the Small Pox," General Alexander Leslie told Lord Charles Cornwallis, commander of the British troops in the south. "I shall distribute them about the Rebell Plantations."[27] One of the worst instances of British betrayal occurred after the Continental Army besieged General Cornwallis and his troops at Yorktown, Virginia, in October 1781. When food and other supplies ran low, the general ordered his men to chase the blacks who had joined him beyond his lines, where almost all either died or were recaptured by the Patriots.[28]

Other British officers maintained the bargain they had struck with former slaves. When Governor Dunmore was forced to abandon the Chesapeake in the summer of 1776, he took along the black recruits who had survived the smallpox epidemic that ravaged his forces. These liberated Virginians spent the war in the New York City area— apparently mostly on Staten Island—joined by thousands of other blacks from up and down the east coast (Document 34). The British-American peace treaty, signed in Paris in September 1783, required British generals to send the slaves who had enlisted with them back to their owners. From his headquarters overlooking the Hudson River, George Washington pressed for their return, including several slaves that he himself claimed to own. British generals such as Guy Carleton, however, ignored Washington's entreaties. During the summer of 1783, a flotilla sailed out of New York City carrying thousands of white Loyalists—and three thousand black ones—into exile.

Although many African Americans were thus able to exploit the fluid conditions of the Revolutionary War in order to gain control of their own destinies, many were not. Especially in the South, armies as well as loosely organized militia bands used the war as an opportunity to seize their enemies' slaves. These stolen men, women, and children, almost always separated from their families, were treated as commodities. Often, when enemy troops seized the slaves from a plantation, the side to which the planter had sworn allegiance—be it Patriot or Loyalist— compensated him with slaves taken from some other plantation. In what was one of the cruelest ironies of the entire war, the Patriot governments of Virginia, Georgia, and the Carolinas all used seized slaves as enlistment bounties. Any white southerner who would join the army of freedom would be compensated with a slave.

FREEDOM, SLAVERY, AND THE REVOLUTIONARY AFTERMATH

The American Revolution liberated thousands of African Americans. Many were able to remain free only by going into exile. But other freedpeople managed to remain in the new United States, where they tried to build communities in the face of hardship and discrimination. Meanwhile, the vast majority of black Americans remained enslaved.

The ideals of the Revolution propelled the early abolition movement forward. Black and white opponents of slavery relentlessly confronted slaveholders with the contradiction between their practices and their ideals. The black petition movement, which had begun before the Revolutionary War, intensified after independence (Documents 20, 21, and 35). One of its leaders was Prince Hall, a free Boston leatherdresser who founded the nation's first black Masonic lodge (which white Masons refused to recognize). He drew up numerous petitions against slavery, in one of which he and other free blacks petitioned the Massachusetts legislature to fund an expedition that would resettle them in Africa (Documents 21 and 26). At least two Massachusetts slaves sued for their freedom in court and won, effectively ending the practice of slavery in that state (Documents 22 and 23). Other New England states and New York, Pennsylvania, and New Jersey adopted gradual emancipation plans that put slavery on the road to extinction. But in most states the process was terribly slow. For instance, Pennsylvania's 1780 emancipation act, adopted partly through the influence of Anthony Benezet (Document 5), did not actually free a single slave. It merely mandated that no one born after its passage could be enslaved (and the sons and daughters of slaves had to serve long apprenticeships before finally receiving their freedom). In New Jersey, the pace of emancipation was even slower; there were still a few slaves in that state as late as 1865. Even the Northwest Ordinance, adopted in 1787 to provide a path to statehood for the white settlements north and west of the Ohio River, prohibited slavery in the region but made an exception for slaveholders who had already settled there with human property.

Farther south, in the Chesapeake states of Delaware, Maryland, and Virginia, a combination of Revolutionary idealism and Christian

piety led state legislatures to allow slaveholders to manumit (emancipate) their human property for the first time. In one of the most dramatic acts of mass emancipation, a fabulously wealthy Virginian,
Robert Carter of Nomini Hall, went through a series of religious con-
versions that culminated in his decision to free all his slaves—nearly
five hundred men, women, and children. But other white people in
these regions feared the presence of free blacks and petitioned their
legislatures to prohibit manumission (Document 25).

Free African Americans had to devote considerable energy to com-
bating whites' race prejudice, which, if anything, increased during the
Revolutionary era. Black almanac author and surveyor Benjamin Banneker publicly challenged Thomas Jefferson's contention that blacks
were inherently inferior (Documents 31 and 32). Black residents of
the new republic also formed self-help groups. For instance, in 1787,
Philadelphia ministers Absalom Jones (1746–1818) and Richard Allen
(1760–1831) took the lead in establishing a Free African Society that
offered its members life insurance and other benefits (Document 27).
In the 1790s, Jones and Allen founded separate black churches, Jones
becoming the first minister of the first black Episcopal church in the
United States (Document 28) and Allen establishing the African
Methodist Episcopal (AME) Church.

The ideology of the American Revolution was so powerful that two
decades later, in 1800, it helped inspire Gabriel's Rebellion, a slave
insurrection conspiracy in Richmond, Virginia. Gabriel, a blacksmith,
and his co-conspirators had not needed the Revolution to teach them
to love liberty. Still, Virginia abolitionist St. George Tucker noted in
the wake of Gabriel's Rebellion that before the Revolution, slaves had
"sought freedom merely as a good; now they also claim it as a right."
"I have nothing more to offer than what General Washington would
have had to offer, had he been taken by the British and put to trial by
them," one of Gabriel's co-conspirators reportedly stated shortly
before he was hanged. "I have adventured my life in endeavouring to
obtain the liberty of my countrymen, and am a willing sacrifice in
their cause."[29] Another conspirator, pressed to testify against Gabriel,
said the slaves had planned to march into Richmond behind a banner
that echoed Patrick Henry by proclaiming the rebels' commitment to
"Death or Liberty" (Document 36). Gabriel himself was hanged in
Richmond on October 10, 1800.

After the Revolutionary War, black Americans who had earned their
freedom by serving the British cause paid the price of going into exile.
Some went to England, others to Bermuda and various British colonies

in the Caribbean, and a few eventually made it as far as Germany and the new British colony in Australia. The greatest number, however, were resettled by the British in Nova Scotia. There tremendous disappointment awaited them. The white Loyalists who settled alongside them were determined to exploit them. The British government pledged that every family of former slaves would, like every white family, receive a farm. But white settlers sought to deprive their black neighbors of economic independence, and they employed ruthless methods to prevent them from redeeming the government's pledge. Soon most of the black Loyalists were working for whites at starvation wages. Many were tricked or coerced into signing long "indentures" that reduced them to a condition akin to slavery (Documents 29, 30, 33, and 34).[30]

The black refugees in Nova Scotia also endured religious persecution. Although some white settlers eagerly participated in the revivals that Baptist minister David George led in and around Shelburne, mobs of whites who disapproved of George's preaching severely beat him and pulled down his house, forcing him to flee (Document 33). Heedless of these dangers, the freeborn John Marrant sailed from London to Nova Scotia in the mid-1780s in order to promote the Methodist faith among the black Loyalists (Document 24).

Even in the face of violent intimidation, black Nova Scotians mounted a series of protests against their deteriorating condition. Eventually Thomas Peters, the one-time Wilmington, North Carolina, millwright who had joined the British army in March 1776, carried their petition to Parliament. In London, he and British abolitionists developed a plan for resettling the exiles in the British colony of Sierra Leone on the west coast of Africa. On January 15, 1792, a fleet of fifteen ships headed east from Nova Scotia carrying some 1,200 former slaves. As they waded ashore in Sierra Leone after a difficult Atlantic crossing during which dozens died, the refugees reportedly sang, "The day of jubilee is come; return ye ransomed sinners home."[31] For Peters, a remarkable odyssey that had started in the hold of a French slave ship had nearly come full circle. He died four months later. David George and Boston King also resettled in Sierra Leone (Documents 33 and 34), and later Captain Paul Cuffe of Massachusetts transported free African Americans to Sierra Leone (Document 37).

One group of African Americans who had escaped to the British chose not to evacuate with them after the war. According to reports that appeared in Georgia and South Carolina newspapers in 1786 and 1787, about three hundred black Loyalists dubbed themselves the "King of England's Soldiers" and found sanctuary in the swampy regions of the lower Savannah River. They formed the nucleus of a maroon (runaway) community that survived several assaults by white militiamen. At least as late as 1787, the year the United States Constitution was written, the beleaguered band of black renegades retained its independence.[32]

The era of the American Revolution was every bit as critical for African Americans as it was for the white Americans who gained independence from Britain, but their story is far less well known. In 1855, black abolitionist William C. Nell recorded the contributions of black Patriots (Document 38), but only in the twenty-first century have historians and others begun to recognize the ways in which the cause of black freedom was intertwined with the movement for American independence. African Americans powerfully influenced the military conflict, and they were powerfully affected by its outcome. Some became free, some were exiled, some gave new momentum to a growing abolition movement, and many remained enslaved in a new nation whose 1787 Constitution endorsed the slave system by providing for the return of runaway slaves and prohibiting a ban on the international slave trade until 1808.

Patriot victory nullified the British ban on settlement beyond the Appalachians, and whites brought plantation slavery to this new region. With the invention of the cotton gin in 1793, cotton became an enormously profitable crop, and the need for agricultural labor was so compelling that white southerners were defending slavery as a positive good by the middle of the nineteenth century. Thus, despite the rhetoric of the Revolution, the new United States developed as a slave nation. The Constitutional Convention gave the southern states bonus representation in the House of Representatives and the electoral college, ensuring their domination of national politics. Even as northern states dismantled slavery, white southerners called on federal troops to put down slave insurrections. The nation divided into free and slave sections, and, by the middle of the nineteenth century, the issue of slavery in a democratic republic came to dominate national politics.

Historian Carl Becker observed in 1909 that there was more to the American War of Independence than the well-known struggle for home rule. The American Revolution was also, he said, a struggle over who would rule at home.[33] Failure to resolve the issues of African American freedom and African American citizenship eventually tore the nation apart. The story of black Americans in the Revolutionary era reveals, to quote twentieth-century author and activist James Baldwin, "more about America to Americans than Americans wish to know."[34]

NOTES

[1]Simon Schama, *Rough Crossings: Britain, the Slaves and the American Revolution* (London: BBC Books, 2005), 7.

[2]Gary B. Nash, *The Forgotten Fifth: African Americans in the Age of Revolution* (Cambridge, Mass.: Harvard University Press, 2006). U.S. Bureau of the Census, *Historical Statistics of the United States, Colonial Times to 1970*, Bicentennial Edition, Part 2 (Washington, D.C.: Government Printing Office, 1975), 1168; Peter H. Wood, "The Changing Population of the Colonial South: An Overview by Race and Region, 1685–1790," in *Powhatan's Mantle: Indians in the Colonial Southeast*, rev. and expanded ed., ed. Peter H. Wood, Gregory A. Waselkov, and Marvin Thomas Hatley (Lincoln: University of Nebraska Press, 2006), 119.

[3]Jupiter Hammon, *A Winter Piece, Being a Serious Exhortation with a Call to the Unconverted* (Hartford, Conn.: Author, 1782), 9, and *An Address to the Negroes, in the State of New-York* (reprinted Philadelphia: Daniel Humphreys, 1787), 10; Sidney Kaplan and Emma Nogrady Kaplan, *The Black Presence in the Era of the American Revolution*, rev. ed. (Amherst: University of Massachusetts Press, 1989), 196, 199.

[4]Benjamin Franklin, "A Conversation between an Englishman, a Scotchman and an American on the Subject of Slavery," quoted in Schama, *Rough Crossings*, 13; Abigail Adams to John Adams, September 22, 1774, in *Adams Family Correspondence*, ed. L. H. Butterfield et al. (8 vol.; Cambridge, Mass.: Harvard University Press, 1963–), 1:162.

[5]Edmund Burke, quoted in Gordon S. Wood, *The Creation of the American Republic, 1776–1787* (Chapel Hill: University of North Carolina Press, 1969), 5; Patrick Henry, quoted in William Wirt Henry, *Patrick Henry: Life, Correspondence, and Speeches* (New York: Charles Scribner's Sons, 1891), 1:266; F. Nwabueze Okoye, "Chattel Slavery as the Nightmare of the American Revolutionaries," *William and Mary Quarterly*, 3rd ser., 37 (1980): 3–28.

[6]Abigail Adams to John Adams, September 22, 1774, in *Adams Family Correspondence*, ed. Butterfield et al. 1:162; James Madison to William Bradford Jr., November 27, 1774, *The Papers of James Madison*, ed. William T. Hutchinson and William M. E. Rachal (Chicago: University of Chicago Press, 1962), 1:130; Peter H. Wood, "'The Dream Deferred': Black Freedom Struggles on the Eve of White Independence," in *In Resistance: Studies in African, Caribbean, and Afro-American History*, ed. Gary Y. Okihiro, (Amherst: University of Massachusetts Press, 1986), 172.

[7]Edmund Randolph, *History of Virginia*, ed. Arthur H. Shaffer (Charlottesville: University Press of Virginia, 1970), 219.

[8]"Deposition of Dr. William Pasteur in Regard to the Removal of Powder from the Williamsburg Magazine," *Virginia Magazine of History and Biography* 13 (1905): 49; Benjamin Waller, deposition, in report of the Committee on the Late Disturbances, June 14, 1775, in *Journals of the House of Burgesses of Virginia, 1773–1776*, ed. John Pendleton Kennedy (Richmond, Va.: E. Waddey Co., 1905), 232; Woody Holton, *Forced Founders: Indians, Debtors, Slaves, and the Making of the American Revolution in Virginia* (Chapel Hill: University of North Carolina Press, 1999), 145, 149.

[9]Quoted in Wood, "'The Dream Deferred,'" 175; Jeffrey J. Crow, "Slave Rebelliousness and Social Conflict in North Carolina, 1775–1802," *William and Mary Quarterly*, 3rd ser., 37 (1980): 83–86; Alan D. Watson, "Impulse toward Independence: Resistance and Rebellion among North Carolina Slaves, 1750–1775," *Journal of Negro History* 63 (1978): 317–28.

[10]Quoted in Sylvia R. Frey, *Water from the Rock: Black Resistance in a Revolutionary Age* (Princeton, N.J.: Princeton University Press, 1991), 58.

[11]Quoted in ibid., 62.

[12]John Drayton, *Memoirs of the American Revolution from Its Commencement to the Year 1776, Inclusive; as Relating to the State of South-Carolina* (1821; reprinted, New York: New York Times and Arno Press, 1969), 1:231.

[13] Holton, *Forced Founders*, 133–34.

[14] Robert Honyman diary, Jan. 1776, Manuscript Division, Library of Congress, Washington, D.C.

[15] Dixon and Hunter's *Virginia Gazette*, Dec. 2, 1775; Benjamin Quarles, *The Negro in the American Revolution* (Chapel Hill: University of North Carolina Press, 1961), 19–32.

[16] Debt owed by Edmund Taylor, "British Mercantile Claims," *Virginia Genealogist* 16 (1972): 104–5.

[17] "MORNING RETURNS of Lord Dunmore's *Black Banditti*," Dixon and Hunter's *Virginia Gazette*, Aug. 31, 1776; Holton, *Forced Founders*, 156.

[18] Quoted in Holton, *Forced Founders*, 159–60.

[19] Quarles, *Negro in the American Revolution*, 69, 71.

[20] Ray Raphael, *A People's History of the American Revolution* (New York: New Press, 2001), 284, 288.

[21] Kaplan and Kaplan, *Black Presence in the American Revolution*, 59.

[22] Ibid., 62.

[23] Gary B. Nash, "Thomas Peters: Millwright and Deliverer," http://revolution.h-net.msu.edu/essays/nash.html.

[24] Schama, *Rough Crossings*, 93.

[25] Quarles, *Negro in the American Revolution*, 144–45.

[26] Todd W. Braisted, "The Black Pioneers and Others: The Military Role of Black Loyalists in the American War of Independence," in *Moving On: Black Loyalists in the Afro-Atlantic World*, ed. John W. Pulis (New York: Garland, 1999), 21.

[27] Alexander Leslie, quoted in Elizabeth A. Fenn, *Pox Americana: The Great Smallpox Epidemic of 1775–82* (New York: Hill and Wang, 2001), 132.

[28] Joseph Plumb Martin, *A Narrative of a Revolutionary Soldier: Some of the Adventures, Dangers, and Sufferings of Joseph Plumb Martin* (1830; reprinted, New York: Signet, 2001), 207.

[29] St. George Tucker, quoted in Joshua Coffin, *An Account of Some of the Principal Slave Insurrections* (New York: American Anti-Slavery Society, 1860), 30; anonymous insurrectionist, quoted in Robert Sutcliff, *Travels in Some Parts of North America, in the Years 1804, 1805, & 1806* (York, England: C. Peacock, 1811), 50.

[30] Schama, *Rough Crossings*, 301.

[31] Quoted in Nash, "Thomas Peters."

[32] Kaplan and Kaplan, *Black Presence in the American Revolution*, 85.

[33] Carl Lotus Becker, *The History of Political Parties in the Province of New York, 1760–1776* (Madison: University of Wisconsin Press, 1909), 22.

[34] James Baldwin, *The Fire Next Time* (New York: Dial Press, 1963), 115.

PART TWO

The Documents

1

Black Americans and the Coming of the American Revolution, 1750–1776

For African Americans, the imperial conflict phase of the American Revolution changed everything and nothing. White leaders who protested British tyranny did not teach enslaved Africans to love liberty, for blacks had always yearned to be free. Yet the Patriot protests of the 1760s and early 1770s did give blacks new opportunities to press their demands and a new language in which to express them. Many documents in this section address liberty. In letters, petitions, pamphlets, and poems, white Patriots and free and enslaved black Americans express their understanding of rights and freedoms. Other documents—newspaper advertisements, a diary, and a memoir—reveal the conditions of black life on the eve of white independence and as the military struggle began.

1

Fugitive Slave Advertisements

1750–1776

Slaves often managed to escape their owners' custody, if only temporarily. When fugitives eluded recapture for more than a few days, their owners typically offered rewards. Notices—similar to the "Wanted" posters seen today in post offices—were affixed outside taverns, in front of court-houses, and wherever colonists gathered. Slaveholders seeking to reclaim their human property also purchased newspaper advertisements like those below. Today's "Wanted" posters have photographs, but in the Revolutionary

Boston Gazette, October 2, 1750; *Virginia Gazette*, July 21, 1774; *Pinkney's Virginia Gazette*, January 6, 1776; *Pennsylvania Gazette*, August 7, 1776.

era, detailed descriptions were necessary, and these provide vivid, if biased, portrayals of slaves. The first advertisement shown here was for the man later known as Crispus Attucks, who was killed in the Boston Massacre of 1770. The last two reveal the ways in which slaves took advantage of the turmoil of war to seek their freedom.

BOSTON GAZETTE

October 2, 1750

RAN–away from his Master *William Brown* of *Framingham*, on the 30th of *Sept.* last, a Molatto[1] Fellow, about 27 Years of Age, named *Crispas*, 6 Feet two inches high, short curl'd Hair, his Knees nearer together than common; had on a light colour'd Bearskin Coat, plain brown Fustian Jacket, or brown all-Wool one, new Buckskin Breeches, blue Yarn Stockings, and a check'd woollen Shirt.

Whoever shall take up said Run-away, and convey him to his above-said Master, shall have *ten Pounds*, old Tenor[2] Reward, and all necessary Charges paid. And all Masters of Vessels and others, are hereby caution'd against concealing or carrying off said Servant on Penalty of the Law. *Boston, October 2, 1750.*

[1]*Molatto*: mulatto, a person of racially mixed ancestry, usually African and European.
[2]*old Tenor*: a form of currency.

PURDIE AND DIXON'S VIRGINIA GAZETTE

July 21, 1774

PORT ROYAL, *June 22, 1774.* RUN away from the Subscriber, a Mulatto Man named GILBERT, five Feet five or six Inches high, by Trade a Shoemaker, has had the Smallpox very bad, the Top of his Head is shaved, and he combs it back like a Woman; he carried off a good many Clothes, so that I cannot describe his Dress. The same Night he absented there went an *Eastern Shore* Vessel down the River, which I expect he got on Board of. It is probable he will change his Name to *Gilbert Morris*, pass for a Freeman, and if possible will try to get out of the Colony. He is a Baptist, and I expect will show a little of it in Company. Any Person that will bring the said Slave to me, near *Port Royal*, shall have 50 s.[3] Reward, besides what the Law allows; and I hereby forewarn all Masters of Vessels from carrying him off, at their Peril.

JOHN EVANS, Senior.

PINKNEY'S VIRGINIA GAZETTE

January 6, 1776

FOURTEEN POUNDS REWARD

RUN away from the subscriber, the 26th of November last, 4 negro men, viz.[4] HARRY, Virginia born, 5 feet 8 or 9 inches high, 30 years of age, a dark mulatto, with long bushy hair; he is of the Indian breed, straight and well made, dresses neat, and has a variety of clothes with him, amongst others, a blue fearnought[5] great coat. He has worked several years at the carpenter's and wheelwright's trade, and can glaize and paint. LEWIS, an outlandish, short, thick fellow, remarkably bow-legged, an excellent wheelwright and waggon maker, and a very good blacksmith. He carried with him, amongst other clothes, a blue suit. AARON, a likely Virginia born fellow, of the middle size, stoops a little, has a hoarse voice, and had on the usual clotheing of negroes. MATTHEW, a Virginia born, dark mulatto, 18 years of age, 5 feet 8 or 9 inches high, stammers a little, and speaks quick, when surprized, and is close-kneed. These 4 went off in a yawl[6] with two others, who have been since committed to the public gaol. As one of them was taken in the yawl without the cape,[7] I conclude the other 4 are in lord Dunmore's service. I will give FIVE POUNDS each for securing the two first, and FORTY SHILLINGS each for the other two, besides what the law allows. They are all outlawed.

EDMUND RUFFIN

PRINCE GEORGE, December 23, 1775.

[3]*s.*: shillings, British currency unit.
[4]*viz.*: namely.
[5]*fearnought*: thick woolen cloth.
[6]*yawl*: small sailing ship.
[7]*without the cape*: outside the mouth of Chesapeake Bay.

PENNSYLVANIA GAZETTE

August 7, 1776

IN MENS CLOTHES

RUN away the 30th of July last, from the Jerseys to Philadelphia or New-York, a MULATTOE Woman Slave, named *Maria*; had on a white or red and white jacket, white ticken breeches, white stockings, old mens shoes, and an old beaver hat; she is hardly discernable from a white woman, is rather thinish visage, middle size, thick legs, long black hair, and about 35 years old; she hath left behind her three young children, a good master and mistress, and is going towards New-York after a married white man, who is a soldier in the Continental service there. Whoever secures the said Mulattoe in goal, and will immediately advertise the same in this paper, shall have FOUR DOLLARS reward.

2

BRITON HAMMON

A Narrative of the Uncommon Sufferings, And Surprizing Deliverance of Briton Hammon, A Negro Man

1760

Briton Hammon's memoir reveals the harsh conditions endured by all Jack Tars, as sailors in Britain's merchant fleet were called, in the years before the American Revolution. It takes the form of a captivity tale, a popular eighteenth-century narrative that more typically told of whites who had been captured by Indians or imprisoned by North African pirates. Hammon's story of being imprisoned in Cuba had a special resonance, since, as he noted on his title page, he was a "Negro" and probably a slave. To what does Hammon attribute his deliverance?

Briton Hammon, *A Narrative of the Uncommon Sufferings, And Surprizing Deliverance of Briton Hammon, A Negro Man* . . . (Boston: Green & Russell, 1760).

A NARRATIVE Of the UNCOMMON SUFFERINGS, AND Surprizing DELIVER-
ANCE OF Briton Hammon, A Negro Man,— —
   Servant to GENERAL WINSLOW, Of *Marshfield*, in NEW-ENGLAND;
Who returned to *Boston*, after having been absent almost Thirteen
Years.
   CONTAINING An Account of the many Hardships he underwent
from the Time he left his Master's House, in the Year 1747, to the
Time of his Return to *Boston*.—How he was Cast away in the Capes of
Florida;—the horrid Cruelty and inhuman Barbarity of the *Indians* in
murdering the whole Ship's Crew;—the Manner of his being carry'd
by them into Captivity. Also, An Account of his being Confined Four
Years and Seven Months in a close Dungeon,—And the remarkable
Manner in which he met with his *good old Master* in *London*; who
returned to *New-England*, a Passenger, in the same Ship.

BOSTON, Printed and Sold by GREEN & RUSSELL, in Queen-Street, 1760.

To THE READER,
   As my Capacities and Condition of Life are very low, it cannot be
expected that I should make those Remarks on the Sufferings I have met
with, or the kind Providence of a good GOD for my Preservation, as one
in a higher Station; but shall leave that to the Reader as he goes along,
and so I shall only relate Matters of Fact as they occur to my Mind—

ON Monday, 25th Day of *December*, 1747, with the leave of my Master,
I went from *Marshfield*, with an Intention to go a Voyage to Sea, and
the next Day, the 26th, got to *Plymouth*, where I immediately ship'd
myself on board of a Sloop, Capt. *John Howland*, Master, bound to
Jamaica and the *Bay*—We sailed from *Plymouth* in a short Time, and
after a pleasant Passage of about 30 Days, arrived at *Jamaica*; we was
detain'd at *Jamaica* only 5 Days, from whence we sailed for the *Bay*,
where we arrived safe in 10 Days. We loaded our Vessel with Log-
wood, and sailed from the *Bay* the 25th Day of *May* following, and the
15th Day of *June*, we were cast away on *Cape-Florida*, about 5 Leagues
from the Shore; being now destitute of every Help, we knew not what
to do or what Course to take in this our sad Condition:—The Captain
was advised, intreated, and beg'd on, by every Person on board, to
heave over but only 20 Ton of the *Wood*, and we should get clear,
which if he had done, might have sav'd his Vessel and Cargo, and not
only so, but his own Life, as well as the Lives of the Mate and Nine
Hands, as I shall presently relate.

After being upon this Reef two Days, the Captain order'd the Boat to be hoisted out, and then ask'd who were willing to tarry on board? The whole Crew was for going on Shore at this Time, but as the Boat would not carry 12 Persons at once, and to prevent any Uneasiness, the Captain, a Passenger, and one Hand tarry'd on board, while the Mate, with Seven Hands besides myself, were order'd to go on Shore in the Boat, which as soon as we had reached, one half were to be Landed, and the other four to return to the Sloop, to fetch the Captain and the others on Shore. The Captain order'd us to take with us our Arms, Ammunition, Provisions and Necessaries for Cooking, as also a Sail to make a Tent of, to shelter us from the Weather; after having left the Sloop we stood towards the Shore, and being within Two Leagues of the same, we espy'd a Number of Canoes, which we at first took to be Rocks, but soon found our Mistake, for we perceiv'd they moved towards us; we presently saw an English Colour[1] hoisted in one of the Canoes, at the Sight of which we were not a little rejoiced, but on our advancing yet nearer, we found them, to our very great Surprize, to be *Indians* of which there were Sixty; being now so near them we could not possibly make our Escape; they soon came up with and boarded us, took away all our Arms Ammunition, and Provision.

The whole Number of Canoes (being about Twenty,) then made for the Sloop, except Two which they left to guard us, who order'd us to follow on with them; the Eighteen which made for the Sloop, went so much faster than we that they got on board above Three Hours before we came along side, and had kill'd Captain *Howland*, the Passenger and the other hand; we came to the Larboard side of the Sloop, and they order'd us round to the Starboard, and as we were passing round the Bow, we saw the whole Number of *Indians*, advancing forward and loading their Guns, upon which the Mate said, "*my Lads we are all dead Men*," and before we had got round, they discharged their Small Arms upon us, and kill'd Three of our hands, viz. *Reuben Young* of *Cape-Cod*, Mate; *Joseph Little* and *Lemuel Doty* of *Plymouth*, upon which I immediately jump'd overboard, chusing rather to be drowned, than to be kill'd by those barbarous and inhuman Savages.

In three or four Minutes after, I heard another Volley which dispatched the other five, viz. *John Nowland*, and *Nathaniel Rich*, both belonging to *Plymouth*, and *Elkanah Collymore*, and *James Webb*, Strangers, and *Moses Newmock*, Molatto. As soon as they had kill'd the whole of the People, one of the Canoes padled after me, and soon

[1] *Colour*: flag.

came up with me, hawled me into the Canoe, and beat me most terribly with a Cutlass, after that they ty'd me down, then this Canoe stood
for the Sloop again and as soon as she came along side, the *Indians* on
board the Sloop betook themselves to their Canoes, then set the Vessel on Fire, making a prodigious shouting and hallowing like so many
Devils. As soon as the Vessel was burnt down to the Water's edge, the
Indians stood for the Shore, together with our Boat, on board of which
they put 5 hands. After we came to the Shore, they led me to their
Hutts, where I expected nothing but immediate Death, and as they
spoke broken English, were often telling me, while coming from the
Sloop to the Shore, that they intended to roast me alive. But the Providence of God order'd it otherways, for He appeared for my Help, *in
this Mount of Difficulty*, and they were better to me then my Fears, and
soon unbound me, but set a Guard over me every Night. They kept
me with them about five Weeks, during which Time they us'd me
pretty well, and gave me boil'd Corn, which was what they often eat
themselves. The Way I made my Escape from these Villains was this;
A Spanish Schooner arriving there from *St. Augustine*, the Master of
which, whose Name was *Romond*, asked the *Indians* to let me go on
board his Vessel, which they granted, and the Captain[2] knowing me
very well, weigh'd Anchor and carry'd me off to the *Havanna*,[3] and
after being there four Days the *Indians* came after me, and insisted on
having me again, as I was their Prisoner;—They made Application to
the Governor, and demanded me again from him; in answer to which
the Governor told them, that as they had put the whole Crew to
Death, they should not have me again, and so paid them Ten Dollars
for me, adding, that he would not have them kill any Person hereafter,
but take as many of them as they could, of those that should be cast
away, and bring them to him, for which he would pay them Ten Dollars a-head. At the *Havanna* I lived with the Governor in the Castle
about a Twelve-month, where I was walking thro' the Street, I met
with a Press-Gang who immediately prest me, and put me into Goal,
and with a Number of others I was confin'd till next Morning, when
we were all brought out, and ask'd who would go on board the King's
Ships, four of which having been lately built, were bound to *Old-Spain*,
and on my refusing to serve on board, they put me in a close Dungeon,
where I was confin'd *Four Years and seven months*; during which Time

[2]The Way I came to know this Gentleman was, by his being taken last War by an
English Privateer, and brought into *Jamaica*, while I was there. [Hammon's note]

[3]*the Havanna*: Havana, Cuba, a Spanish colony, where Hammon was held as a prisoner and slave for more than seven years.

I often made application to the Governor, by Persons who came to see the Prisoners, but they never acquainted him with it, nor did he know all this Time what became of me, which was the means of my being confin'd there so long. But kind Providence so order'd it, that after I had been in this Place so long as the Time mention'd above the Captain of a Merchantman, belonging to *Boston*, having sprung a Leak was obliged to put into the *Havanna* to refit, and while he was at Dinner at Mrs. *Betty Howard's*, she told the Captain of my deplorable Condition, and said she would be glad, if he could by some means or other relieve me; The Captain told Mrs. *Howard* he would use his best Endeavours for my Relief and Enlargement.

Accordingly, after Dinner, came to the Prison, and ask'd the Keeper if he might see me; upon his Request I was brought out of the Dungeon, and after the Captain had Interrogated me, told me, he would intercede with the Governor for my Relief out of that miserable Place, which he did, and the next Day the Governor sent an Order to release me; I lived with the Governor about a Year after I was delivered from the Dungeon, in which Time I endeavour'd three Times to make my Escape, the last of which proved effectual; the first Time I got on board of Captain *Marsh*, an *English* Twenty Gun Ship, with a Number of others, and lay on board conceal'd that Night; and the next Day the Ship being under sail, I thought myself safe, and so made my Appearance upon Deck, but as soon as we were discovered the Captain ordered the Boat out, and sent us all on Shore—I intreated the Captain to let me, in particular, tarry on board, begging, and crying to him, to commiserate my unhappy Condition, and added, that I had been confin'd almost five Years in a close Dungeon, but the Captain would not hearken to any Intreaties, for fear of having the Governor's Displeasure, and so I was obliged to go on Shore.

After being on Shore another Twelvemonth, I endeavour'd to make my Escape the second Time, by trying to get on board of a Sloop bound to *Jamaica*, and as I was going from the City to the Sloop, was unhappily taken by the Guard, and ordered back to the Castle, and there confined.—However, in a short Time I was set at Liberty, and order'd with a Number of others to carry the[4] *Bishop* from the Castle, thro' the Country, to confirm the old People, baptize Children, &c.[5] for which he receives large Sums of Money.—I was employ'd in this

---

[4]He is carried (by Way of Respect) in a large Two-arm Chair; the Chair is lin'd with crimson Velvet, and supported by eight Persons. [Hammon's note]

[5]&c.: etc.

Service about Seven Months, during which Time I lived very well, and then returned to the Castle again, where I had my Liberty to walk about the City, and do Work for my self;—The *Beaver*, an *English* Man of War then lay in the Harbour, and having been informed by some of the Ship's Crew that she was to sail in a few Days, I had nothing now to do, but to seek an Opportunity how I should make my Escape.

Accordingly one Sunday Night the Lieutenant of the Ship with a Number of the Barge Crew were in a Tavern, and Mrs. *Howard* who had before been a Friend to me, interceded with the Lieutenant to carry me on board: the Lieutenant said he would with all his Heart, and immediately I went on board in the Barge. The next Day the *Spaniards* came along side the *Beaver*, and demanded me again, with a Number of others who had made their Escape from them, and got on board the Ship, but just before I did; but the Captain, who was a true *Englishman*, refus'd them, and said he could not answer it, to deliver up any *Englishmen* under *English* Colours.—In a few Days we set Sail for *Jamaica*, where we arrived safe, after a short and pleasant Passage.

After being at *Jamaica* a short Time we sail'd for *London*, as convoy to a Fleet of Merchantmen, who all arrived safe in the *Downs*, I was turned over to another Ship, the *Arcenceil*, and there remained about a Month. From this Ship I went on board the *Sandwich* of 90 Guns; on board the *Sandwich*, I tarry'd 6 Weeks, and then was order'd on board the *Hercules*, Capt. *John Porter*, a 74 Gun Ship, we sail'd on a Cruize, and met with a *French* 84 Gun Ship, and had a very smart Engagement,[6] in which about 70 of our Hands were Kill'd and Wounded, the Captain lost his Leg in the Engagement, and I was Wounded in the Head by a small Shot. We should have taken this Ship, if they had not cut away the most of our Rigging; however, in about three Hours after, a 64 Gun Ship, came up with and took her.—I was discharged from the *Hercules* the 12th Day of *May* 1759 (having been on board of that Ship 3 Months) on account of my being disabled in the Arm, and render'd incapable of Service, after being honourably paid the Wages due to me. I was put into the *Greenwich* Hospital where I stay'd and soon recovered.—I then ship'd myself a Cook on board Captain *Martyn*, an arm'd Ship in the King's Service. I was on board this Ship almost Two Months, and after being paid my Wages, was discharg'd in the Month of *October*.—After my discharge from Captain *Martyn*, I was taken

---

[6]A particular Account of this Engagement, has been Publish'd in the *Boston* News-Papers. [Hammon's note]

sick in *London* of a Fever, and was confin'd about 6 Weeks, where I expended all my Money, and left in very poor Circumstances; and unhappy for me I knew nothing of my *good Master's* being in *London* at this my very difficult Time. After I got well of my sickness, I ship'd myself on board of a large Ship bound to *Guinea*, and being in a publick House one Evening, I overheard a Number of Persons talking about Rigging a Vessel bound to *New-England*, I ask'd them to what Part of *New-England* this Vessel was bound? they told me, to *Boston*; and having ask'd them who was Commander? they told me, Capt. *Watt*; in a few Minutes after this the Mate of the Ship came in, and I ask'd him if Captain *Watt* did not want a Cook, who told me he did, and that the Captain would be in, in a few Minutes; and in about half an Hour the Captain came in, and then I ship'd myself at once, after begging off from the Ship bound to *Guinea*; I work'd on board Captain *Watt's* Ship almost Three Months, before she sail'd, and one Day being at Work in the Hold, I overheard some Persons on board mention the Name of *Winslow*, at the Name of which I was very inquisitive, and having ask'd what *Winslow* they were talking about? They told me it was *General Winslow*; and that he was one of the Passengers, I ask'd them what *General Winslow*? For I never knew *my good Master*, by that Title before; but after enquiring more particularly I found it must be *Master*, and in a few Days Time the Truth was joyfully verify'd by a happy Sight of his Person, which so overcome me, that I could not speak to him for some Time—*My good Master* was exceeding glad to see me, telling me that I was like one arose from the Dead, for he thought I had been Dead a great many Years, having heard nothing of me for almost Thirteen Years.

I think I have not deviated from Truth, in any particular of this my Narrative, and tho' I have omitted a great many Things, yet what is wrote may suffice to convince the Reader, that I have been most grievously afflicted, and yet thro' the Divine Goodness, as miraculously preserved, and delivered out of many Dangers; of which I desire to retain a *grateful Remembrance*, as long as I live in the World.

And now, That in the Providence of that GOD, *who delivered his Servant* David out of the Paw of the Lion and out of the Paw of the Bear, *I am freed from a* long *and* dreadful Captivity, among worse Savages than they; *And am return'd to my* own Native Land, to Shew how Great Things the Lord hoth done for Me; *I would call upon all Men, and Say*, O Magnifie the Lord with Me, and let us Exalt his Name together!— O that Men would Praise the Lord for His Goodness, and for his Wonderful Works to the Children of Men!

3

JAMES OTIS

The Rights of the British Colonies Asserted and Proved

1764

One of the most frequently reprinted and widely circulated pamphlets of the American Revolution was also one of the first. James Otis (1725–1783) published The Rights of the British Colonies Asserted and Proved *in 1764, a year before Parliament adopted the hated Stamp Act. During the early years of the imperial conflict, many writers based the British Americans' privileges—such as freedom from parliamentary taxation—on their colonial charters (constitutions) or their rights as Englishmen. Otis, a Boston, Massachusetts, attorney, dug deeper. In his view, the colonists derived their liberties from the natural rights that belonged to all human beings. This contention, which was quickly adopted by other American writers, forced Otis to confront the issue of slavery.*

The Colonists are by the law of nature free born, as indeed all men are, white or black. No better reasons can be given, for enslaving those of any color than such as baron Montesquieu[1] has humorously given, as the foundation of that cruel slavery exercised over the poor Ethiopians; which threatens one day to reduce both Europe and America to the ignorance and barbarity of the darkest ages. Does it follow that tis[2] right to enslave a man because he is black? Will short curl'd hair like wool, instead of christian hair, as tis called by those, whose hearts are as hard as the nether millstone, help the argument? Can any logical inference in favour of slavery, be drawn from a flat nose, a long or a short face. Nothing better can be said in favor of a trade, that is

---

[1]*Baron Montesquieu*: Charles-Louis de Secondat, baron de Montesquieu (1689–1755), a French political philosopher who was well-regarded in the English-speaking world.

[2]*tis*: it is.

James Otis, *The Rights of the British Colonies Asserted and Proved* (Boston: Edes & Gill, 1764), 29–30.

the most shocking violation of the law of nature, has a direct tendency to diminish the idea of the inestimable value of liberty, and makes every dealer in it a tyrant, from the director of an African company to the petty chapman[3] in needles and pins on the unhappy coast. It is a clear truth, that those who every day barter away other mens liberty, will soon care little for their own. . . .

The Colonists being men, have a right to be considered as equally entitled to all the rights of nature with the Europeans, and they are not to be restrained in the exercise of any of these rights, but for the evident good of the whole community.

By being or becoming members of society, they have not renounced their natural liberty in any greater degree than other good citizens, and if tis taken from them without their consent, they are so far enslaved.

[3]*chapman*: peddler.

4

LANDON CARTER

Plantation Diary

March 22, 1770

Landon Carter (1710–1778) was one of the wealthiest men in Virginia, the most populous of Britain's North American colonies. Carter inherited dozens of black Virginians from his father and from the three wives he outlived. In his diaries, he left a more extensive record of his plantation management than did any other Virginian of the colonial era. The entries often record his struggles with his slaves.

Colonel Fauntleroys feast day where I suppose my family must go.

We have heapd our dung at [Mangorike,] the mud house & the barn. Those people are finishing the hoeing their new Corn field but

From Carter Family Papers, Alderman Library, University of Virginia, Charlottesville.

up here Dolman tho 3 days at it has not finishd heaping the dung in the Cow yard quite and has the Tob[acco house] & sheep house to do.

Guy came home yesterday and had his correction[1] for run away in sight of the people. The 2 sarahs came up yesterday pretending to be violent ill with pains in their sides. They look very well[,] had no fever[,] and I order'd them down to their work upon pain of a whipping. They went[,] workd very well with no grunting about pain but one of them to wit[2] Manuels sarah taking the advantage of Lawsons ride to the fork swore she would not work any longer & run away and is still out. There is a curiosity in[3] this Creature. She worked none last year pretending to be with Child & this she was full 11 months before she was brot to bed.[4] She has now the same pretence & thinks to pursue the same course but as I have full warning of her deceit if I live I will break her of that trick. I had two before of this turn. Wilmot of the fork whenever she was with Child always pretended to be too heavy to work and it cost me 12 months before I broke her. Criss of Mango[rik]e fell into the same scheme & really carried it to a great length for at last she could not be dragged out. However by carrying a horse with traces the Lady took to her feet run away & when catched by a severe whipping has been a good slave ever since only a cursed thief in making her Children milk my Cows in the night. . . .

[1] *correction*: punishment, usually whipping.
[2] *to wit*: namely.
[3] *a curiosity in*: something curious about.
[4] *was bro[ugh]t to bed*: went into labor.

5

ANTHONY BENEZET

Some Historical Account of Guinea ... with an Inquiry into the Rise and Progress of the Slave Trade, Its Nature and Lamentable Effects

1771

Anthony Benezet (1713–1784) was born in San Quentin, France, to wealthy Huguenot (Protestant) parents. His family emigrated to London and then to Philadelphia, where Benezet joined the Society of Friends, or Quakers, a religious group that opposed slavery. After a brief and unsatisfying career as a merchant, he became a teacher and textbook author. Benezet threw himself into a host of reform campaigns, but starting in the early 1750s, his great cause became the abolition of slavery. He played an instrumental role in persuading Philadelphia's Quaker association to denounce slavery and eventually, in 1776, to disown all Quakers who refused to free their slaves. Benezet's most powerful weapon against slavery was a series of carefully researched books and pamphlets. One of the most influential was Some Historical Account of Guinea, *in which he not only exposed the cruelties of human bondage but also refuted one of the most persuasive justifications for it: the notion that Africans were too intellectually stunted to provide for themselves without European direction. The excerpt below follows Benezet's account of the "Middle Passage"—the transportation of enslaved Africans across the Atlantic Ocean. After describing the sale of the transported Africans, Benezet offers his proposal for gradual emancipation. How does he support it? How might African Americans have reacted to Benezet's plan?*

When the vessels arrive at their destined port in the colonies, the poor Negroes are to be disposed off to the planters, and here they are again exposed naked, without any distinction of sexes, to the brutal examination of their purchasers; and this, it may well be judged, is to many

From Anthony Benezet, *Some Historical Account of Guinea, Its Situation, Produce, and the General Disposition of Its Inhabitants, with an Inquiry into the Rise and Progress of the Slave-Trade, Its Nature and Lamentable Effects* ... (Philadelphia: Joseph Crukshank, 1771), 128–29, 138–44.

another occasion of deep distress. Add to this, that near connections must now again be separated to go with their several purchasers; this must be deeply affecting to all, but such whose hearts are seared by the love of gain. Mothers are seen hanging over their daughters, bedewing their naked breasts with tears, and daughters clinging to their parents, not knowing what new stage of distress must follow their separation, or whether they shall ever meet again. And here what sympathy! What commiseration do they meet with! Why, indeed, if they will not separate as readily as their owners think proper, the Whipper is called for, and the lash is exercised upon their naked bodies, till obliged to part. Can any human heart, which is not become callous by the practise of such cruelties, be unconcerned, even at the relation of such grievous affliction, to which this oppressed part of our species are subjected. . . .

It is scarce to be doubted, but that the foregoing accounts will beget in the heart of the considerate readers, an earnest desire to see a stop put to this complicated evil, but the objection with many is, What shall be done with those Negroes already imported and born in our families? Must they be sent to Africa? That would be to expose them in a strange land to greater difficulties than many of them labour under at present. To set them suddenly free here, would be, perhaps, attended with no less difficulty; for undisciplined as they are in religion and virtue, they might give a loose to those evil habits, which the fear of a master would have restrained. These are objections which weigh with many well disposed people, and it must be granted these are difficulties in the way; nor can any general change be made or reformation affected without some; but the difficulties are not so great but that they may be surmounted. If the government was so considerate of the iniquity and danger attending on this practice as to be willing to seek a remedy, doubtless, the Almighty would bless this good intention, and such methods would be thought of, as would not only put an end to the unjust oppression of the Negroes, but might bring them under regulations that would enable them to become profitable members of society. For the furtherance of which, the following proposals are offered to consideration: That all farther importation of slaves be absolutely prohibited; and as to those born amongst us, after serving so long as may appear to be equitable, let them by law be declared free. Let every one thus set free, be enrolled in the county courts, and be obliged to be a resident during a certain number of years within the said county, under the care of the overseers of the poor.[1] Thus being,

---

[1] *the overseers of the poor*: part-time government officials charged with providing relief to impoverished residents.

in some sort, still under the direction of governors and the notice of those who were formerly acquainted with them, they would be obliged to act the more circumspectly, and make proper use of their liberty, and their children would have an opportunity of obtaining such instruction as is necessary to the common occasions of life, and thus both parents and children might gradually become useful members of the community. And further, where the nature of the country would permit, as certainly the uncultivated condition of our southern and most western colonies easily would: suppose a small tract of land were assigned to every Negroe family, and they obliged to live upon and improve it, (when not hired out to work for the white people) this would encourage them to exert their abilities and become industrious subjects. Hence both planters and tradesmen would be plentifully supplied with chearful and willing minded labourers, much vacant land would be cultivated; the produce of the country be justly encreased; the taxes for the support of government lessened to individuals by the encrease of taxables. And the Negroes, instead of being and object of Terror,[2] as they certainly must be to the governments where their numbers are great, would become interested in their safety and welfare. . . .

It is frequently offered as an argument in vindication of the use of Negroe slaves. That the warmth of the climate in the West Indies,[3] will not permit white people to labour in the culture of the land; but upon an acquaintance with the nature of the climate, and its effects upon such labouring white people as are prudent and moderate in labour and the use of spirituous liquors, this will be found to be a mistaken opinion. Those islands were, at first, wholly cultivated by white men; the encouragement they then met with for a long course of years was such as occasioned a great encrease of people. Richard Ligon, in his history of Barbadoes, where he resided from the year 1647 to 1650, about 24 years after its first settlement, writes, "that there was then fifty thousand souls on that island, besides Negroes; and that though the weather was very hot, yet not so scalding, but that servants, both Christians and slaves laboured ten hours a day." By other accounts we gather, that the white people have since decreased to less than one

---

[2]The hard usage the Negroes meet with in the plantations, and the great disproportion between them and the white people, will always be a just cause of terror. In Jamaica and some parts of South-Carolina, it is supposed that there are fifteen blacks to one white. [Benezet's note]

[3]*West Indies*: Caribbean islands such as Barbados and Jamaica.

half the number which was there at that time; and by relations of the first settlements of the other islands, we do not meet with any complaints of unfitness in the white people for labour there, before slaves were introduced. The island of Hispaniola,[4] which is one of the largest of those islands, was at first planted by the Bucaneers,[5] a set of hardy laborious men, who continued so for a long course of years, till following the example of their neighbours in the purchase and use of Negroe Slaves, idleness and excess prevailing, debility and disease naturally succeeded, and have ever since continued. If, under proper regulations, liberty was proclaimed through the colonies, the Negroes, from a dangerous grudging half-fed slaves, might become able willing minded Labourers. And if there was not a sufficient number of these to do the necessary work, a competent number of labouring people might be procured from Europe, which affords numbers of poor distressed objects, who, if not overlooked, with proper usage, might, in several respects, better answer every good purpose in performing the necessary labour in the islands than the slaves now do.

A farther considerable advantage might accrue to the British nation in general, if the slave trade was laid aside, by the cultivation of a fair, friendly and humane commerce with the Africans, without which it is not possible the inland trade of that country should ever be extended to the degree it is capable of; for while the spirit of butchery and making slaves of each other is promoted by the Europeans amongst the Negroes, no mutual confidence can take place; nor will the Europeans be able to travel with safety into the heart of their country to form and cement such commercial friendships and alliances as might be necessary to introduce the arts and sciences amongst them, and engage their attention to instruction in the principles of the Christian religion, which is the only sure foundation of every social virtue. Africa has about ten thousand miles of sea coast, and extends in depth near three thousand miles from east to west, and as much from north to south; stored with vast treasures of materials necessary for the trade and manufactures of Great-Britain, and from its climate and the fruitfulness of its soil, capable, under proper management, of producing, in the greatest plenty, most of the commodities which are imported into Europe from those parts of America subject to the English government,

---

[4]*Hispaniola*: the largest island in the Caribbean Sea, now divided between Haiti and the Dominican Republic.
[5]*Bucaneers*: buccaneers, pirates preying on the Spanish treasure fleets carrying gold and silver from the Americas to Europe.

and as in return they would take our manufactures, the advantages of this trade would soon become so great, that it is evident this subject merits the regard and attention of the government.

6

FELIX

Petition to Governor, Council, and House of Representatives of Massachusetts

January 6, 1773

The author of this petition prudently chose to sign it using his first name only, but he made a wide variety of religious and secular arguments against slavery. Most historians presume that Felix was Felix Holbrook, an African American who also signed an antislavery letter to the Massachusetts legislature (see Document 8). In this petition, what did he ask for?

To His Excellency THOMAS HUTCHINSON, Esq; GOVERNOR;
To The Honorable His Majesty's COUNCIL, and
To the Honorable House of REPRESENTATIVES in General Court[1] assembled at BOSTON, the 6th Day of *January*, 1773.

The humble PETITION of many SLAVES, living in the Town of BOSTON, and other Towns in the Province is this, namely,

THAT your EXCELLENCY and Honors, and the Honorable the Representatives would be pleased to take their unhappy State and Condition under your wise and just Consideration.

WE desire to bless GOD, who loves Mankind, who sent his Son to die for their Salvation, and who is no Respecter of Persons; that he hath lately put it into the Hearts of Multitudes on both Sides of the Water,[2] to bear our Burthens, some of whom are Men of great

[1] *General Court*: Massachusetts legislature.
[2] *the Water*: the Atlantic Ocean.

The Appendix: Or, Some Observations on the Expediency of the Petition of the Africans . . . (Boston: E. Russell, 1773), 9–11.

Note and Influence; who have pleaded our Cause with Arguments which we hope will have their weight with this Honorable Court.

WE presume not to dictate to your EXCELLENCY and Honors, being willing to rest our Cause on your Humanity and Justice; yet would beg Leave to say a Word or two on the Subject.

ALTHOUGH some of the Negroes are vicious, (who doubtless may be punished and restrained by the same Laws which are in Force against other of the King's Subjects) there are many others of a quite different Character, and who, if made free, would soon be able as well as willing to bear a Part in the Public Charges;[3] many of them of good natural Parts, are discreet, sober, honest, and industrious; and may it not be said of many, that they are virtuous and religious, although their Condition is in itself so unfriendly to Religion, and every moral Virtue except *Patience*. How many of that Number have there been, and now are in this Province, who have had every Day of their Lives imbittered with this most intollerable Reflection, That, let their Behaviour be what it will, neither they, nor their Children to all Generations, shall ever be able to do, or to possess and enjoy any Thing, no, not even *Life itself*, but in a Manner as the *Beasts that perish*.

WE have no Property! We have no Wives! No Children! We have no City! No Country! But we have a Father in Heaven, and we are determined, as far as his Grace shall enable us, and as far as our degraded contemptuous Life will admit, to keep all his Commandments: Especially will we be obedient to our Masters, so long as GOD in his sovereign Providence shall *suffer* us to be holden in Bondage.

IT would be impudent, if not presumptuous in us, to suggest to your Excellency and Honors any Law or Laws proper to be made, in relation to our unhappy State, which, although our greatest Unhappiness, is not our *Fault*; and this gives us great Encouragement to pray and hope for such Relief as is consistent with your Wisdom, Justice, and Goodness.

WE think ourselves very happy, that we may thus address the Great and General Court of this Province, which great and good Court is to us, the best Judge, under GOD, of what is wise, just, and good.

WE humbly beg Leave to add but this one Thing more: We pray for such Relief only, which by no Possibility can ever be productive of the least Wrong or Injury to our Masters; but to us will be as Life from the dead.

Signed,

FELIX

---

[3] *Public Charges*: government expenses.

7

PATRICK HENRY

Letter to Robert Pleasants

January 18, 1773

Virginian Patrick Henry (1736–1799) is most famous for his 1775 "Give me liberty or give me death" speech. Two years before that oration, Henry discussed whether enslaved African Americans also had the right to be free. In this letter to fellow Virginian Robert Pleasants, a Quaker who had sent him a book by Quaker Anthony Benezet (see Document 5), Henry agrees that blacks do deserve freedom, but he goes on to say that he has no plans to free any of his own slaves.

Dear Sir Hannover January 18th 1773

I take this oppertunity to acknoledge the receipt of Anthony Benezet's Book against the slave trade,[1] I thank you for it. It is not a little surprising that Christianity, whose Chief Excellence consists, in softning the Human Heart, in Cherishing and Improving its finer feelings should incourage a practice so totally repugnant to the first Impressions of right and wrong, what adds to the wonder is, that this abominable practice has been Introduced in the most Enlightened ages, times that seems to have Pretentions to boast of high Improvements in arts sciences and refined morality, have brought into general use, and guarded by many Laws a Spieces[2] of violence & tyranny which our more rude and barbarous, but more Honest ancestors detested.

Is it not amazing that at a time when the rights of Humanity are defined and understood with precision in a Country above all others fond of Liberty, that in such an age, and such a Country, we find men professing a Religion, the most humane, mild, meek gentle and generous, adopting a principle as repugnant to Humanity as it is Inconsistant with the Bible and destructive to Liberty. Every thinking Honest

---

[1]*Anthony Benezet's Book against the slave trade*: possibly a reference to Benezet's *Some Historical Account of Guinea* (Document 5).

[2]*Spieces*: species, sort.

Granville Sharp Letterbook, Library Company of Philadelphia.

man rejects it in speculation, how few in practice from Conscientious motives. The world in general has denied your people[3] a share of its Honours, but the wise will ascribe to you a just tribute of virtuous praise for the practice of a train of virtues among which your disagreement to Slavery will be principaly ranked. I cannot but wish well to a people whose system Imitates the Example of him whose life was perfect,[4] and believe mee I shall Honour the Quakers for their noble Effort to abolish Slavery. It is Equally calculated to promote moral and political good.

Would any one believe that I am Master of Slaves of my own purchase. I am drawn along by the general Inconveniancy of living without them. I will not, I cannot justify it; However culpable my Conduct I will so far pay my duty as to own the Excellence and rectitude of her precepts and lament my want of conformity to them.

I believe a time will come when an opertunity will be offered to abolish this lamentable Evil, every thing we can do is to Improve it, if it happens in our day, if not let us transmit to our Decendants together with our Slaves, a pitty for their unhappy lot and an abhorance for Slavery. If we cannot reduce this wished for Reformation to practice let us treat the unhappy Victims with Lenity. It is the farthest advance we can make towards justice. It is a debt we owe to the purity of our religion to shew that it is at variance with that Law Which warrants Slavery. Here is an Instance that silent meetings the scoff of reverend doctors have done that which learned and Elaborate preaching could not Effect. So much preferable are the genuine dictates of Conscience and a steady attention to its feelings, above the teachings of those men who pretend to have found a better guide. I Exhort you to persevere in so worthy a resolution. Some of your people disagree or at least are lukewarm in the abolition of Slavery. Many treat the resolutions of your meeting with ridicule and among those who throw contempt on it, are Clergymen, whose surest guard against both ridicule and contempt is a certain act of assembly. I know not where to stop. I could say many things on this subject, a serious review of which gives a gloomy perspective to future times. Excuse this scrawl and believe me with Esteem.

Your Humble Servant
PATRICK HENRY JUNR

---

[3]*your people*: Quakers.
[4]*him whose life was perfect*: Jesus Christ.

8

PETER BESTES AND OTHER MASSACHUSETTS SLAVES

Letter to Local Representatives

April 20, 1773

White colonists' protests often charged that the policies adopted by King George III and Parliament took away their liberty and even threatened to "enslave" them. The Patriots' use of this sort of rhetoric provided an opening for enslaved African Americans. Blacks called on white Americans to be consistent, to grant all their fellow British subjects, regardless of skin color, the same freedom they sought to preserve for themselves. As colonial protests escalated, this new argument against slavery, based on the natural rights of man, took its place alongside the older claim that slavery violated Christian principles. Notice that the letter writers acknowledge their obligations to their masters—but on what basis? Notice, too, that they propose to return to Africa. What are they asking for?

The letter below was printed so that African Americans throughout the province of Massachusetts could send copies to their members of the General Court, the colonial legislature.

BOSTON, APRIL *20th, 1773*

SIR,

THE efforts made by the legislative of this province in their last sessions to free themselves from slavery,[1] gave us, who are in that deplorable state, a high degree of satisfaction. We expect great things from men who have made such a noble stand against the designs of their *fellow-men* to enslave them. We cannot but wish and hope Sir, that you will have the same grand object, we mean civil and religious liberty, in view in your next session. The divine spirit of *freedom*, seems to fire every humane breast on this continent, except such as are bribed to assist in executing the execrable plan.

[1] *to free themselves from slavery:* Patriots said British officials who sought to enforce taxes and regulations on them were in effect trying to enslave them.

Printed Broadside ([Boston?], 1773).

46

WE are very sensible that it would be highly detrimental to our present masters, if we were allowed to demand all that of *right* belongs to us for past services; this we disclaim. Even the *Spaniards*, who have not those sublime ideas of freedom that English men have, are conscious that they have no right to all the services of their fellow-men, we mean the *Africans*, whom they have purchased with their money; therefore they allow them one day in a week to work for themselve, to enable them to earn money to purchase the residue of their time, which they have a right to demand in such portions as they are able to pay for (a due appraizment of their services being first made, which always stands at the purchase money).[2] We do not pretend to dictate to you Sir, or to the honorable Assembly, of which you are a member: We acknowledge our obligations to you for what you have already done, but as the people of this province seem to be actuated[3] by the principles of equity and justice, we cannot but expect your house[4] will again take our deplorable case into serious consideration, and give us that ample relief which, *as men*, we have a natural right to.

BUT since the wise and righteous governor of the universe,[5] has permitted our fellow men to make us slaves, we bow in submission to him, and determine to behave in such a manner, as that we may have reason to expect the divine approbation of, and assistance in, our peaceable and lawful attempts to gain our freedom.

WE are willing to submit to such regulations and laws, as may be made relative to us, until we leave the province, which we determine to do as soon as we can from our joynt labours procure money to transport ourselves to some part of the coast of *Africa*, where we propose a settlement. We are very desirous that you shou'd have instructions relative to us, from your town, therefore we pray you to communicate this letter to them, and ask this favor for us.

In behalf of our fellow slaves in this province,

And by order of their Committee.

PETER BESTES,
SAMBO FREEMAN,
FELIX HOLBROOK,
CHESTER JOIE.

---

[2]*stands at the purchase money*: set at the price the owner paid for the slaves, that is, the Spanish allowed slaves to buy their freedom if they could come up with the amount their owners had paid for them.

[3]*actuated*: motivated.

[4]*house*: legislative body.

[5]*governor of the universe*: God.

9

PHILLIS WHEATLEY

Poems on Various Subjects, Religious and Moral

1773

Phillis Wheatley was born in the Gambia River region of West Africa in about 1753. Around the age of fourteen, she was kidnapped and sold into slavery. She ended up in Boston, Massachusetts, where she was sold to John and Susanna Wheatley, who taught her to read. She started writing poetry and in 1773 became the first African American ever to publish a book, Poems on Various Subjects, Religious and Moral. *The first poem reprinted below, which she wrote in 1770, commemorates the death of George Whitefield (1714–1770), a traveling evangelical minister whose passionate preaching won him fame and converts throughout Britain and its colonies in North America. Wheatley witnessed one of his sermons shortly before his death. In the second poem, first published in her 1773 book, Wheatley seems to celebrate her enslavement, since it led to her conversion to Christ. But note her instruction to white Christians in the poem's last four lines. What is she asking them to remember? Wheatley was freed in 1773 and died eleven years later.*

On the Death of the Rev. Mr. George Whitefield

1770

HAIL, happy saint, on thine immortal throne,
Possest of glory, life, and bliss unknown;
We hear no more the music of thy tongue,
Thy wonted auditories[1] cease to throng.
Thy sermons in unequall'd accents flow'd,
And ev'ry bosom with devotion glow'd;
Thou didst in strains of eloquence refin'd

---

[1] *Thy wonted auditories*: your usual audiences.

Phillis Wheatley, *Poems on Various Subjects, Religious and Moral* (London: A. Bell, 1773), 22–24.

Inflame the heart, and captivate the mind.
Unhappy we the setting sun deplore,
So glorious once, but ah! it shines no more.

Behold the prophet in his tow'ring flight!
He leaves the earth for heav'n's unmeasur'd height,
And worlds unknown receive him from our sight.

There *Whitefield* wings with rapid course his way,
And sails to *Zion* through vast seas of day.
Thy pray'rs, great saint, and thine incessant cries
Have pierc'd the bosom of thy native skies.
Thou moon hast seen, and all the stars of light,
How he has wrestled with his God by night.
He pray'd that grace in ev'ry heart might dwell,
He long'd to see *America* excel;
He charg'd its youth that ev'ry grace divine
Should with full lustre in their conduct shine;
That Saviour, which his soul did first receive,
The greatest gift that ev'n a God can give,
He freely offer'd to the num'rous throng,
That on his lips with list'ning pleasure hung.

"Take him, ye wretched, for your only good,
"Take him ye starving sinners, for your food;
"Ye thirsty, come to this life-giving stream,
"Ye preachers, take him for your joyful theme;
"Take him my dear *Americans*, he said,
"Be your complaints on his kind bosom laid:
"Take him, ye *Africans*, he longs for you,
"*Impartial Saviour* is his title due:
"Wash'd in the fountain of redeeming blood,
"You shall be sons, and kings, and priests to God."

Great *Countess*,[2] we *Americans* revere
Thy name, and mingle in thy grief sincere;
New England deeply feels, the *Orphans* mourn,
Their more than father will no more return.

But, though arrested[3] by the hand of death,
Whitefield no more exerts his lab'ring breath,

---

[2]The Countess of *Huntingdon*, to whom Mr. *Whitefield* was Chaplain. [Wheatley's note]
[3]*arrested*: halted.

Yet let us view him in th' eternal skies,
Let ev'ry heart to this bright vision rise;
While the tomb safe retains its sacred trust,
Till life divine re-animates his dust.

On Being Brought from Africa to America
1773

'TWAS mercy brought me from my *Pagan* land,
Taught my benighted soul to understand
That there's a God, that there's a *Saviour* too:
Once I redemption neither sought nor knew.
Some view our sable[4] race with scornful eye,
"Their colour is a diabolic die."
Remember, *Christians*, *Negros*, black as *Cain*,
May be refin'd,[5] and join th' angelic train.

[4]*sable*: black.
[5]*refin'd*: civilized, cultured.

10

PHILLIS WHEATLEY

Letter to Samson Occom
February 11, 1774

Phillis Wheatley's letter to Samson Occom, a Mohegan Indian who had become a Presbyterian minister and missionary, contains a much more powerful denunciation of slavery than any of her poems. Like other African Americans, Wheatley calls attention to the "strange Absurdity" of white protests for liberty that ignore the liberty of black Americans. Like many black and white abolitionists, she bases African Americans' claims

Massachusetts Gazette, March 24, 1774.

on the same natural rights principles that were invoked by the American revolutionaries. The letter was not intended as a private statement; it was printed in a dozen newspapers.

Rev'd and honor'd Sir,

I Have this Day received your obliging kind Epistle, and am greatly satisfied with your Reasons respecting the Negroes, and think highly reasonable what you offer in Vindication of their natural Rights: Those that invade them cannot be insensible that the divine Light is insensibly chasing away the thick Darkness which broods over the Land of Africa; and the Chaos which has reign'd so long, is converting into beautiful Order, and reveals more and more clearly, the glorious Dispensation of civil and religious Liberty, which are so inseparably united, that there is little or no Enjoyment of one without the other. Otherwise, perhaps the Israelites had been less solicitous for their Freedom from Egyptian Slavery; I don't say they would have been contented without it, by no Means, for in every human Breast, God has implanted a Principle, which we call Love of Freedom; it is impatient of Oppression, and pants for Deliverance; and by the leave of our modern Egyptians[1] I will assert, that the same Principle lives in us. God Grant Deliverance in his own Way and Time, and get him honour upon all those whose Avarice impels them to countenance and help forward the Calamities of their fellow Creatures. This I desire not for their Hurt, but to convince them of the strange Absurdity of their Conduct whose Words and Actions are so diametrically opposite. How well the Cry for Liberty, and the reverse Disposition for the exercise of oppressive Power over others agree—I humbly think it does not require the Penetration of a Philosopher to determine.

[1] *by the leave of our modern Egyptians*: with the permission of our owners. Wheatley is referring, with irony, to the biblical story of the Hebrews' enslavement in Egypt.

11

ANDREW ESTAVE

Letter in Pinkney's Virginia Gazette

July 20, 1775

In July 1775, the Revolutionary War had not yet come to Virginia, but New England farmers had already fought British regulars at Lexington, Concord, and Bunker Hill. Free Virginians were beginning to divide into two camps: a small band of Loyalists led by Lord Dunmore, the royal governor, and a much larger group of Patriots. Within the expanding breach between white Patriots and Loyalists, enslaved Virginians found opportunity. One such slave was a fifteen-year-old who had been accused of a horrific crime. She hoped to receive sanctuary at the governor's palace in Williamsburg, the provincial capital. But Governor Dunmore had left the palace shortly before she tried to reach him.

As the public have lately entertained a very disadvantageous opinion of me with regard to my usage of a negro wench, about fifteen years of age, whom I had of Mr. *Malory*, it gives me the greatest pain imaginable to be reduced to the disagreeable necessity of being troublesome to the public on this occasion. But as there is nothing more sacred and dear to one than his reputation and character in the world, I humbly hope that this consideration will have its due weight with the public, and be a sufficient advocate for my trespassing on their time and patience.

Since the 10th of February, 1775, at which time this wench came into my possession, she has eloped from my service no less than thirteen times, without the least shadow of a provocation. For the three first times I gave her to the number of forty lashes, but all to no purpose. At last, seeing it was of no avail to correct her any more, I gave her entirely over to herself, to see if this usage would have any effect upon her stubborn nature; since which she has often run off, and been brought back to me, without receiving the least correction, although she had robbed me of two silver coffee spoons, in company with her husband, who had run off along with her. Since her last return she has continued with me for the space of fifteen days; during which time my little daughter, about three years of age, fell into a lingering disorder, the cause of which we could not discover, she continuing to cry incessantly. One day my negro woman[1] found my child, together with this cruel and unnatural wretch, concealed behind my barn, among the bushes, with her thumb thrust into the private parts of my poor child. She being struck with horror at the sight, ran in immediately to acquaint us. We accordingly found the little innocent all over bloody, and in a most terrible condition. During the confusion we were put in by this accident she took the opportunity of making her escape, and made to the palace.[2] When brought from thence I gave her eighty lashes, well laid on, and afterwards applied to her back a handful of cold embers; for which I have been stigmatized with the epithets[3] of cruel and inhuman; but I leave it to the impartial public, if, in this situation, I acted beyond the bounds of humanity, in the extremity a father must be in upon seeing his innocent child used in this manner.

ANDREW ESTAVE

[1] *my negro woman*: another of Estave's slaves.
[2] *made to the palace*: headed to the Governor's Palace in Williamsburg.
[3] *stigmatized with the epithets*: branded with the insulting terms.

12

JOHN MURRAY, LORD DUNMORE

A Proclamation
November 7, 1775

In 1775, after hostilities broke out in Massachusetts, very few white people in Virginia, the largest of the thirteen colonies, became Loyalists. Yet 40 percent of the colony's population was enslaved, and even before the war started, black Virginians began to send messages to Lord Dunmore, the British colonial governor, offering to help suppress the Patriot insurgency in return for their freedom. At first, Dunmore, himself a

By His Excellency the Right Honourable John Earl of Dunmore . . . (Norfolk, Va.: John H. Holt, 1775).

slaveowner, turned them away, but eventually the governor, whose troops were vastly outnumbered, began quietly admitting the slaves who made it to his lines. On November 7, 1775, Dunmore drew up a proclamation that offered freedom to any Patriot's slave who would fight for the king. He issued it eight days later. The same document that stirred black Virginians' dreams of freedom infuriated their owners and drove many white neutralists and even Loyalists into the Patriot camp. Indeed, many whites who had refused to embrace the cause of independence now declared their willingness to separate from the British Empire.

By His Excellency the Right Honorable JOHN Earl of DUNMORE, His MAJESTY's Lieutenant and Governor General of the Colony and Dominion of VIRGINIA, and Vice Admiral of the same.

A PROCLAMATION.

As I have ever entertained Hopes that an Accommodation[1] might have taken Place between GREAT-BRITAIN and this Colony, without being compelled by my Duty to this most disagreeable but now absolutely necessary Step, rendered so by a Body of armed Men unlawfully assembled, firing on His MAJESTY's Tenders,[2] and the formation of an Army, and that Army now on their March to attack His MAJESTY's Troops and destroy the well disposed Subjects of this Colony. To defeat such treasonable Purposes, and that all such Traitors, and their Abettors,[3] may be brought to Justice, and that the Peace, and good Order of this Colony may be again restored, which the ordinary Course of the Civil Law is unable to effect; I have thought fit to issue this my Proclamation, hereby declaring, that until the aforesaid good Purposes can be obtained, I do in Virtue of the Power and Authority to ME given, by His MAJESTY, determine to execute Martial Law, and cause the same to be executed throughout this Colony: and to the end that Peace and good Order may the sooner be restored, I do require every Person capable of bearing Arms, to resort to His MAJESTY's STANDARD,[4] or be looked upon as Traitors to His MAJESTY's Crown and Government, and thereby become liable to the Penalty the Law

---

[1] *Accommodation*: truce.
[2] *Tenders*: support ships.
[3] *Abettors*: helpers.
[4] *His Majesty's standard*: the king's flag, symbol of royal authority.

inflicts upon such Offences; such as forfeiture of Life, confiscation of Lands, &c. &c. And I do hereby further declare all indented Servants, Negroes, or others, (appertaining to Rebels,) free that are able and willing to bear Arms, they joining His MAJESTY's Troops as soon as may be, for the more speedily reducing this Colony to a proper Sense of their Duty, to His MAJESTY's Crown and Dignity. I do further order, and require, all His MAJESTY's Liege Subjects, to retain their Quitrents,[5] or any other Taxes due or that may become due, in their own Custody, till such Time as Peace may be again restored to this at present most unhappy Country, or demanded of them for their former salutary Purposes, by Officers properly authorised to receive the same.

GIVEN under my Hand on board the Ship WILLIAM, off NORFOLK, the 7th Day of NOVEMBER, in the SIXTEENTH Year of His MAJESTY's Reign.

DUNMORE.

(GOD save the KING.)

[5] *Quitrents*: nominal rent that all landowners had to pay.

13

THOMAS JEFFERSON

Original Rough Draft of the Declaration of Independence

June 1776

In the spring of 1776, with hostile clashes in several colonies and King George III declaring the colonies to be in a state of rebellion, the Continental Congress began to seriously consider declaring independence. A committee was appointed to prepare a declaration, and Thomas Jefferson was asked to draft it. In his original draft, Jefferson accused King George of waging "a cruel war against human nature" by capturing Africans and

Thomas Jefferson Papers, Manuscript Division, Library of Congress, Washington, D.C.

carrying them into slavery. Jefferson criticized the king for never suppressing "this execrable commerce" and for now stirring up slave revolts in the colonies. Look carefully at the words Jefferson used to describe King George's actions. These words did not survive the Continental Congress's review and editing of the Declaration, which claims in its final form only that the king "has excited domestic insurrections amongst us." Why do you think the Congress made the final document much less specific and direct? To what did the phrase "domestic insurrections" refer?

[H]e has waged cruel war against human nature itself, violating it's most sacred rights of life & liberty in the persons of a distant people who never offended him, captivating & carrying them into slavery in another hemisphere, or to incure miserable death in their transportation thither.[1] This piratical warfare, the opprobium of <u>infidel</u> powers,[2] is the warfare of the <u>Christian</u> king of Great Britain, determined to keep open a market where MEN should be bought & sold he has prostituted his negative[3] for suppressing every legislative attempt to prohibit or to restrain this execrable commerce and that this assemblage of horrors might want no fact of distinguished die, he is now exciting those very people to rise in arms among us, and to purchase that liberty of which he has deprived them, by murdering the people upon whom <u>he</u> also obtruded[4] them: thus paying off former crimes committed against the <u>liberties</u> of one people, with crimes which he urges them to commit against the <u>lives</u> of another.

---

[1] *thither*: there.
[2] *infidel powers*: non-Christian governments.
[3] *negative*: veto.
[4] *obtruded*: imposed.

2

Black Americans in Military Service, 1775–1783

Within the widening gap between white Loyalists, who remained loyal to King George III and the British government, and Patriots, the supporters of Jefferson's Declaration of Independence, thousands of enslaved African Americans found opportunities to obtain their own freedom.

Some who fought on the Patriot side, in local militias and in the Continental Army, received freedom for their service. Many more escaped their owners and made their way to the nearest British ship or army camp, for the British declared that slaves who joined them would be free. On both sides, African Americans served as guides, spies, and soldiers, but most were only allowed to perform unskilled labor. Some served in all-black regiments, while others were attached to regular army units.

The following documents include reports and letters about black military service in both armies as well as applications for pensions made long after the war. Memoirs in the final section of documents also include information on black military service.

14

A Letter from Monmouth County
June 21, 1780

This extract from an announcement in a Pennsylvania newspaper offers a glimpse of the actions of whites and African Americans who participated in raids and other forms of guerrilla warfare. One group of Loyalist raiders, led by a black man variously known as Titus, Tye, and Ty, conducted punishing raids on Patriot farms and villages. These earned its commander the honorific title "Colonel Tye." Tye's so-called Black Brigade (which was actually biracial) was based at Sandy Hook, New Jersey, at the entrance to New York harbor. In the incident described here, the group attacked the region from which Tye had fled slavery, Monmouth County, New Jersey. Late in the war, Tye was killed by a group of Patriot guerrillas similar to his own Loyalist band.

"Ty, with his party of about 20 blacks and whites, last Friday afternoon took and carried off prisoners, Capt. Barns Smock and Gilbert Vanmater; at the same time spiked up the iron four pounder[1] at Capt. Smock's house, but took no ammunition: Two of the artillery horses, and two of Capt. Smocks's horses, were likewise taken off."

The above-mentioned Ty is a Negroe, who bears the title of Colonel, and commands a motly[2] crew at Sandy-Hook.

[1]*spiked up the iron four pounder*: destroyed the cannon capable of firing four-pound balls.
[2]*motly*: multicolored.

From *Pennsylvania Gazette*, June 21, 1780.

15

SERGEANT MURPHY STEELE

Deposition Reporting
a Supernatural Encounter

August 16, 1781

Like most other British American colonists, African Americans frequently combined a strong Christian faith with an abiding belief in the power and presence of the supernatural. Both convictions appear to have contributed to an incident involving Murphy Steele (or Stiel), a sergeant in the Black Pioneers, an all-black British army unit created during the Revolutionary War. At the time, Steele was stationed in New York City.

August 16th
  1781.

Murphy Stiel of the Black Pioneers Says, That about a fortnight ago at Noon, when he was in the Barracks of the Company in Water Street, he heard a Voice like a Man's (but saw no body) which called him by his name, and desired him to go and tell The Commander in Chief, Sir Henry Clinton, to send word to Genl. Washington That he must Surrender himself and his Troops to the King's Army, and that if he did not the wrath of God would fall upon them.

That if General Washington did not Surrender, The Commr. in Chief was then to tell him, that he would raise all the Blacks in America to fight against him. The Voice also said that King George must be acquainted with the above.

That the same Voice repeated the aforesaid Message to him several times afterwards and three days ago in Queen Street insisted that he should tell it to Sir Henry Clinton, upon which he answered that he was afraid to do it, as he did not see the Person that spoke. That the Voice then said that he must tell it, that he was not to see him for that he was the Lord, and that he must acquaint Sir Henry Clinton that it

Henry Clinton Papers, volume 170, Item 27, Clements Library, University of Michigan, Ann Arbor.

was the Lord that spoke this; and to tell Sir Henry also, that he and Lord Cornwallis was to put an end to this Rebellion, for that the Lord would be on their Side.

16

JOHN TRUMBULL

The Death of General Warren at the Battle of Bunker's Hill (Detail)

1786

John Trumbull (1756–1843) served in the Continental Army during the early years of the Revolutionary War and later painted portraits of Patriot heroes and memorialized the war with historical paintings of battle scenes. Despite the racial prejudices of his time, Trumbull made no effort to cover up the fact that African Americans made major contributions to the war effort. In his famous depiction of the Battle of Bunker Hill, which had taken place just north of Boston on June 17, 1775, Trumbull gave prominent attention to Peter Salem, a free black man who had enlisted in the Patriot cause. Trumbull's painting was officially entitled The Death of General Warren at the Battle of Bunker's Hill. *To provide a detailed look at how Trumbull depicted Salem, a detail of the far right portion of Trumbull's painting is reproduced here.*

17

SAUL

Petition to the Virginia State Legislature, with Endorsement

October 9, 1792

A Virginian named Saul was among the thousands of African Americans who enlisted in the Continental Army. He not only served with distinction in the American forces but took advantage of the British army's eagerness for African American recruits to travel behind enemy lines as spies. Notice Saul's thoughts about British war aims. When Saul asked the Virginia General Assembly to reward his service — presumably with freedom and a military pension — he included an endorsement from his commanding officer, a white man named Josiah Parker.

To the Honourable the Speaker, and Members of the General Assembly.

The Petition of Saul, a black slave, the property of Geo. Kelly Esqr., Humbly sheweth.

In the beginning of the late war, that gave America Independence, your Petitioner shouldered his muskit and repaired to the american standard. Regardless of the Invitation, trumpeted forth by British Proclamations, for slaves to Emancipate themselves, by becoming the assassins of their owners, your Petitioner avoided the rock that too many of his colour were shipwreck'd on. He was taught to know, that war was levied upon America, not for the Emancipation of Blacks, but for the subjugation of Whites, and he thought the number of Bondmen ought not to be augmented; Under those impressions, your Petitioner did actually campaign it in both Armies — In the American Army, as a soldier, In the British Army, as a spy, which will more fully appear, reference being had to certificates of officers of respectability.

Virginia Legislative Petitions, Norfolk County, Box 181, Folder 65, Library of Virginia, Richmond.

In this double profession, your Petitioner flatters himself that he ren
dered essential service to his country, and should have rendered
much more, had he not, in the Campaign of 1781, been betrayed by a
Negro whom the British had employed upon the same business in Genl.
Mulenburg's Camp. Your Petitioner was at the time, in Portsmouth, a
British Garrison, collecting Information for Colonel Josiah Parker, and
his heels sav'd his neck. He flew to the advanc'd Post, commanded by
Col Parker, and that very night led down the party, as a guide, who
took off the British Picquett.[1]

[1] *Picquett*: picket, one or more soldiers stationed in front of an army in order to gain
advance notice of enemy attacks.

18

JACOB FRANCIS

Pension Application

1836

*Despite Commander in Chief George Washington's initial attempt to ban
all African Americans from the Continental Army, eventually all of the
northern states grew so desperate for recruits that they permitted slaves
to gain their freedom by enlisting. In the nineteenth century, after the
majority of the Revolutionary War soldiers had died, Congress finally
authorized pensions for the surviving veterans. Applicants were required
to describe their military service.*

*Jacob Francis was born in Hunterdon County, New Jersey, in 1754
and died in 1836, shortly after filing his pension application. For reasons that are unclear (his mother may have been free), he was a servant,
not a slave, and he had already received his freedom when he enlisted
in October 1775. Here he describes his service in New England and*

John C. Dann, ed., *The Revolution Remembered: Eyewitness Accounts of the War for Independence* (Chicago: University of Chicago Press, 1980), 391–99.

New York and during the famous crossing of the Delaware on Christmas night 1776. He also records a common soldier's complaint—lack of regular pay.

I was born in the township of Amwell, in the county of Hunterdon, on the fifteenth January, 1754. I never had or saw any record of my age. I learned it from my mother and the persons with whom I lived my time till I was of age, as I always understood I was bound by my mother, a colored woman, when I was young to one Henry Wambough (or Wambock) in Amwell. He parted with me to one Michael Hatt. He sold my time[1] to one Minner Gulick (called Hulick), a farmer in Amwell. He sold my time when I was a little over thirteen years of age to one Joseph Saxton. He went in the spring of the year 1768 and took me with him as his servant to New York, from thence to Long Island, where we took shipping[2] in May 1768 and went to the island of St. John's. We visited different parts of that island and spent the summer there. Towards fall we came to the town of St. Peter's, where we took shipping and returned to Salem, Massachusetts, where we arrived about the month of November 1769. In Salem, Mr. Saxton sold my time to one Benjamin Deacon, with whom I was to serve six years and until I was twenty-one years of age. With him I lived and served in Salem until my time was out, which was in January 1775.

I lived in Salem and worked for different persons till the fall of 1775. In the spring of that year the war had commenced, and the battles of Bunker Hill and Lexington had taken place. About the last of October, I enlisted as a soldier in the United States service for one year. . . .

In 1776, after the British left Boston, the army, with our regiment and myself along with them, marched by way of Roxbury (that way we could go by land) over a causeway into Boston and lay over two or three days, then were ordered out to Bunker Hill. We marched out and encamped there and lay there some time. Then our regiment was ordered to an island at that time called Castle William. The island contained about ten acres. It was about three leagues, or nine miles from Boston. The channel for vessels passed close under it. The island had had a fortification in the shape of a half moon, but it was pretty much

---

[1] *my time*: the remaining years I was required to serve.
[2] *took shipping*: embarked on a ship.

destroyed by the British before they left. The British fleet then lay about nine miles farther out. We lay on that island till about harvest-time. Then we left the island and was ordered to New York from the island. We crossed the river, left Boston on our right hand, and marched to New London. There we took shipping and come to New York. Came down the East River; left Long Island on our left. The British was then on Long Island. At that time the people were culling oats. We stayed a day or two in New York. There were no other troops but our regiment with us. After a day or two, we marched out to a place called Hell Gate, on the north side of the East River. There we threw up breastworks,[3] and the British threw up breastworks on Long Island on the opposite side of the East River and used to fire across. We lay there some time.

While we lay there, the Battle of Long Island took place. There was a number of men detailed from our regiment, so many from each company, to go over and join the American army, perhaps two hundred men. I was one. We crossed the river at Hell Gate and marched on to the island in the direction we was ordered, but did not get to join the army till the battle had commenced and our army was on the retreat. We had to cross a creek to get to our army, who had engaged the enemy on the other side, but before we got to that creek our army was repulsed and retreating, and many of them were driven into the creek and some drowned. The British came in sight, and the balls flew round us, and our officers, finding we could do no good, ordered us to retreat, which we did under the fire of the enemy. We retreated back to Hell Gate and recrossed to our fortifications. Soon after that, we had orders to leave that place and marched to Westchester by way of Kingsbridge. We lay there some time, and every night we had a guard stationed out two or three miles from where the regiment lay at a place called Morrisania. I mounted guard there every time it came to my turn. There was an island near there. The tide made up round it. The British had a station on the island, and a British ship lay there. In an attack on the island one night, Colonel Jackson was wounded. After some time, we were ordered to march to the White Plains. We marched there and there joined General Washington's army.

We lay some time at the White Plains. While we lay there, the British landed and attacked some of our troops and had a brush there. Our regiment and I with them marched by General Washington's orders toward a hill where the engagement was, but the British got

[3] *breastworks*: dirt wall used as fortification.

possession of the hill, and we retreated back to the camp. The British established a garrison on that hill. I stood sentinel that night in a thicket between the American camp and the hill, so near the British lines that I could hear the Hessians in the garrison, which was between one-quarter and one-half mile from me. The British lay there awhile and then left that place, and our regiments marched after them about three or four miles farther east. Then we received orders and marched to Peekskill on the North[4] River. We halted a day and night a little distance from the river and there crossed at Peekskill to the west side of the river. From thence we marched on, and I do not recollect the names of places we passed through till we got to Morristown, New Jersey. We lay there one night, then marched down near to Baskingridge and lay there the next night. That night General Lee was taken[5] in or about Baskingridge. I heard the guns firing. The next morning we continued our march across Jersey to the Delaware and crossed over to Easton. From thence we marched down the Pennsylvania side into Bucks County.

It was then cold weather, and we were billeted[6] about in houses. Our company lay off from the river a few miles below Corvell's Ferry and above Howell's Ferry. We lay there a week or two; then we received orders to march and, Christmas night, crossed the river[7] and marched down to Trenton early in the morning. Our regiment crossed at Howell's Ferry, four miles above Trenton and marched down the River Road and entered the west end of the town. General Washington with the rest of the army crossed at McKonkey's Ferry, four miles above Howell's, and marched down the Scotch Road and came into the north end of the town. We marched down the street from the River Road into the town to the corner where it crosses the street running up towards the Scotch Road and turned up that street. General Washington was at the head of that street coming down towards us and some of the Hessians between us and them. We had the fight. . . . After about half an hour the firing ceased, and some officers, among whom I recollect was General Lord Stirling, rode up to Colonel Sergeant and conversed with him. Then we were ordered to follow them, and with these officers and Colonel Sergeant at our head, we marched

---

[4]*North*: Hudson.
    [5]*General Lee was taken*: the American general Charles Lee was captured by the British.
    [6]*billeted*: housed.
    [7]*crossed the river*: the December 25, 1776, event immortalized in Emanuel Leutze's painting, *Washington Crossing the Delaware*.

down through the town toward Assanpink and up the Assanpink on the north side of it and to the east of the town, where we were formed in line and in view of the Hessians, who were paraded on the south side of the Assanpink and grounded their arms[8] and left them there and marched down to the old ferry below the Assanpink, between Trenton and Lamberton.

Soon after that, a number of men from our regiment were detailed to go down and ferry the Hessians across to Pennsylvania. I went as one, and about noon it began to rain and rained very hard. We were engaged all the afternoon ferrying them across till it was quite dark, when we quit. I slept that night in an old mill-house above the ferry on Pennsylvania side. The next morning I joined my regiment where I had left them the day before up the Assanpink, east of Trenton. We lay there a day or two, and then the time of the year's men was out, and our regiment received part of their pay and were permitted to return home. I did not get a discharge. At that time I had seven and a half months' pay due to me, and I believe others had the same. I received three months' pay, and all the rest of the regiment received the same, and we were ordered after a certain time to come to Peekskill on the North River, and then we should receive our pay and get our discharges. I was with the regiment and in service from the time of enlistment till that time about fourteen months and never left it until I had received the three months' pay and had permission to return to the place of my nativity in Amwell, about fifteen miles from Trenton. I immediately returned to Amwell and found my mother living, but in ill health. I remained with her, and when the time came to go to Peekskill for my pay and discharge, I gave up going and never received either my pay or a discharge in writing. That pay, four and one-half months at forty shillings a month (nine pounds proclamation money equal to twenty-four dollars), is yet due to me from the United States. . . .

I recollect other occasions when I was out, although I cannot state them exactly in their order of time. I was out in the militia at the time of the Battle of Brandywine. I was at Newark at the time Lord Cornwallis was taken. I am not able to state the times and places of my services more particularly, but I am satisfied that the time I served in the militia added to the time I served in the Continental army considerably exceeds the span of two years. I have no discharge or documentary evidence to know my services or assist my memory.

---

[8]*grounded their arms*: placed their muskets on the ground.

19

JEHU GRANT

Pension Application, with Corroborating Letter
1836

Jehu Grant escaped his owner, a Loyalist Rhode Islander, and enlisted as a teamster in a Connecticut unit of the Continental Army. Teamsters were in charge of the teams of animals that pulled wagons containing army supplies. Despite his service, he was eventually returned to his owner, obtaining his freedom only later. Because Grant had technically been an escaped slave, Commissioner of Pensions J. L. Edwards denied Grant's first application. Grant wrote him again with additional reasons why he deserved a pension. This time he also included a letter in which he attempted to corroborate his claim.

That he was a slave to Elihu Champlen who resided at Narraganset, Rhode Island. At the time he left him his said master was called a Tory and in a secret manner furnished the enemy when shipping lay nearby with sheep, cattle, cheese, etc., and received goods from them. And this applicant[1] being afraid his said master would send him to the British ships, ran away sometime in August 1777, as near as he can recollect, being the same summer that Danbury was burnt. That he went right to Danbury after he left his said master and enlisted to Capt. Giles Galer for eighteen months. That, according to the best of his memory, General Huntington and General Meigs's brigades, or a part of them, were at that place. That he, this applicant, was put to teaming with a team of horses and wagon, drawing provisions and various other loading for the army for three or four months until winter set in, then was taken as a servant to John Skidmore, wagon master general (as he was called), and served with him as his waiter until spring, when the said troops went to the Highlands or near that place on the Hudson River, a little above the British lines. That this applicant had

[1]*this applicant*: Jehu Grant.

John C. Dann, ed., *The Revolution Remembered: Eyewitness Accounts of the War for Independence* (Chicago: University of Chicago Press, 1980), 27–28.

charge of the team as wagoner and carried the said General Skidmore's baggage and continued with him and the said troops as his wagoner near the said lines until sometime in June, when his said master either sent or came, and this applicant was given up to his master again, and he returned, after having served nine or ten months.

[Grant wishes] to state that he forwarded to the War Department a declaration founded on the Pension Act of June 1832 praying to be allowed a pension (if his memory serves him) for ten months' service in the American army of the Revolutionary War. That he enlisted as a soldier but was put to the service of a teamster[2] in the summer and a waiter in the winter. In April 1834 I received a writing from Your Honor, informing me that my "services while a fugitive from my master's service was not embraced in said Act," and that my "papers were placed on file." In my said declaration, I just mentioned the cause of leaving my master, as may be seen by a reference thereunto, and I now pray that I may be permitted to express my feelings more fully on that part of my said declaration.

I was then grown to manhood, in the full vigor and strength of life, and heard much about the cruel and arbitrary things done by the British. Their ships lay within a few miles of my master's house, which stood near the shore, and I was confident that my master traded with them, and I suffered much from fear that I should be sent aboard a ship of war. This I disliked. But when I saw liberty poles and the people all engaged for the support of freedom, I could not but like and be pleased with such thing (God forgive me if I sinned in so feeling). And living on the borders of Rhode Island, where whole companies of colored people enlisted, it added to my fears and dread of being sold to the British. These considerations induced me to enlist into the American army, where I served faithful about ten months, when my master found and took me home. Had I been taught to read or understand the precepts of the Gospel, "Servants obey your masters," I might have done otherwise, notwithstanding the songs of liberty that saluted my ear, thrilled through my heart. But feeling conscious that I have since compensated my master for the injury he sustained by my enlisting, and that God has forgiven me for so doing, and that I served my country faithfully, and that they having enjoyed the benefits of my service to an equal degree for the length [of] time I

---

[2]*teamster*: manager of a team of horses or oxen pulling a cart.

served with those generally who are receiving the liberalities of the government, I cannot but feel it becoming me to pray Your Honor to review my declaration on file and the papers herewith amended.

A few years after the war, Joshua Swan, Esq., of Stonington purchased me of my master and agreed that after I had served him a length of time named faithfully, I should be free. I served to his satisfaction and so obtained my freedom. He moved into the town of Milton, where I now reside, about forty-eight years ago. After my time expired with Esq. Swan, I married a wife. We have raised six children. Five are still living. I must be upward of eighty years of age and have been blind for many years, and, not withstanding the aid I received from the honest industry of my children, we are still very needy and in part are supported from the benevolence of our friends. With these statements and the testimony of my character herewith presented, I humbly set my claim upon the well-known liberality of government.

Most respectfully your humble servant

his
JEHU ✠ GRANT
mark

3

Freedom, Slavery,
and the Revolutionary Aftermath,
1775–1800

Enslaved African Americans had always yearned to be free, and the American Revolution gave thousands of them an opportunity to pursue that dream. As the documents in the previous section showed, military service was the means by which most gained their freedom. Others, however, demanded that white Patriots confront the contradiction between their denunciations of British tyranny and their oppression of African Americans. Blacks asserted their rights in a variety of ways. They signed petitions, filed lawsuits, and wrote stirring meditations on the meaning of freedom.

White responses to these African American assertions were as diverse as the demands themselves. Some whites boldly acknowledged that freedom was every person's right, or Christian duty, and some acted on that belief. Others responded with bold new defenses of human bondage. Some found justification in the Bible; others said Africans and their American descendants were an inferior race that could not survive on its own.

The new U.S. Constitution, written in 1787, not only failed to end slavery but bolstered it. In the south, slaves continued to escape and rebel. In the north, free black people struggled to build their own communities in the face of discrimination. Those black men and women who had sided with the British received their freedom, but only in exile; many resettled in Nova Scotia and some eventually moved to Africa.

20

NERO BREWSTER AND OTHER
NEW HAMPSHIRE SLAVES

Petition to the New Hampshire Legislature
November 12, 1779

African Americans seeking freedom employed a wide variety of rhetorical tactics, many of which can be seen in this petition, which explicitly asks for freedom. The African American petitioners appealed to the legislators' Christianity and their patriotism, and they invoked the principle of natural rights. As you read, look for echoes of the Declaration of Independence. The slaves also made a point that would be emphasized over and over again by abolitionists in the nineteenth century: that slavery often led to the permanent dissolution of families. Note that the signatures affixed to the petition indicate influence not only from England but also from the Bible, ancient Greece and Rome (it was common for owners to give their slaves classical names), and even from Africa.

To the Honorable, the Council and House of Representatives of said state, now sitting at Exeter in and for said state:

The petition of the subscribers, natives of Africa, now forcibly detained in slavery in said state, most humbly *sheweth*,[1] That the *God* of Nature gave them life and freedom, upon the terms of the most perfect equality with other men; That freedom is an inherent right of the human species, not to be surrendered, but by consent, for the sake of social life; That private or public tyranny and slavery are alike detestable to minds conscious of the equal dignity of human nature; That in power and authority of individuals, derived solely from a principle of coertion, against the will of individuals, and to dispose of their persons and properties, consists the completest idea of private and political slavery; That all men being amenable to the Deity for the ill-improvement of

---

[1]*sheweth*: shows, proclaims.

Isaac W. Hammond, ed., "Slavery in New Hampshire," *Magazine of American History* 21 (1889): 63–64.

the blessings of His Providence, they hold themselves in duty bound strenuously to exert every faculty[2] of their minds to obtain that blessing of freedom, which they are justly entitled to from that donation of the beneficent Creator; That through ignorance and brutish violence of their native countrymen, and by the sinister designs of others (who ought to have taught them better), and by the avarice of both, they, while but children, and incapable of self-defence, whose infancy might have prompted protection, were seized, imprisoned, and transported from their native country, where (though ignorance and unchristianity prevailed) they were born free, to a country, where (though knowledge, Christianity and freedom are their boast) they are compelled and their posterity to drag on their lives in miserable servitude: Thus, often is the parent's cheek wet for the loss of a child, torn by the cruel hand of violence from her aching bosom; Thus, often and in vain is the infant's sigh for the nurturing care of its bereaved parent, and thus do the ties of nature and blood become victims to cherish the vanity and luxury of a fellow mortal. Can this be right? Forbid it gracious Heaven!

Permit again your humble slaves to lay before this honorable assembly some of those grievances which they daily experience and feel. Though fortune hath dealt out our portion with rugged hand, yet hath she smiled in the disposal of our persons to those who claim us as their property; of them we do not complain, but from what authority they assume the power to dispose of our lives, freedom and property, we would wish to know. Is it from the sacred volume of Christianity? There we believe it is not to be found; but here hath the cruel hand of slavery made us incompetent judges, hence knowledge is hid from our minds. Is it from the volumes of the laws? Of these also slaves cannot be judges, but those we are told are founded on reason and justice; it cannot be found there. Is it from the volumes of nature? No, here we can read with others, of this knowledge, slavery cannot wholly deprive us; here we know that we ought to be free agents; here we feel the dignity of human nature; here we feel the passions and desires of men, though checked by the rod of slavery; here we feel a just equality; here we know that the God of nature made us free. Is their authority assumed from custom? If so let that custom be abolished, which is not founded in nature, reason nor religion. Should the humanity and benevolence of this honorable

---

[2]*faculty*: ability, skill.

assembly restore us that state of liberty of which we have been so long deprived, we conceive that those who are our present masters will not be sufferers by our liberation, as we have most of us spent our whole strength and the prime of our lives in their service; and as freedom inspires a noble confidence and gives the mind an emulation to vie in the noblest efforts of enterprise, and as justice and humanity are the result of your deliberations, we fondly hope that the eye of pity and the heart of justice may commiserate our situation, and put us upon the equality of freemen, and give us an opportunity of evincing to the world our love of freedom by exerting ourselves in her cause, in opposing the efforts of tyranny and oppression over the country in which we ourselves have been so long injuriously enslaved.

Therefore, Your humble slaves most devoutly pray for the sake of injured liberty, for the sake of justice, humanity and the rights of mankind, for the honor of religion and by all that is dear, that your honors would graciously interpose in our behalf, and enact such laws and regulations, as you in your wisdom think proper, whereby we may regain our liberty and be ranked in the class of free agents, and that the name of slave may not more be heard in a land gloriously contending for the sweets of freedom. And your humble slaves as in duty bound will ever pray.

Portsmouth Nov. 12, 1779.

NERO BREWSTER	PHARAOH ROGERS	ROMEO RINDGE
SENECA HALL	CATE NEWMARCH	PETER WARNER
CESAR GERRISH	PHARAOH SHORES	ZEBULON GARDNER
WINSOR MOFFATT	QUAM SHERBURNE	GARRETT COTTON
SAMUEL WENTWORTH	KITTRIDGE	WILL CLARKSON
PETER FROST	TUCKERMAN	PRINCE WHIPPLE
CIPIO HUBBARD	JACK ODIORNE	

21

JOHN CUFFE AND OTHER FREE BLACKS FROM DARTMOUTH

Petition to the Massachusetts Legislature

February 10, 1780

Most African Americans who obtained their freedom faced intense discrimination. For example, several states, including Massachusetts, at times denied free black men (along with all women and also white men who did not own a certain amount of property) the right to vote. A group of African Americans in the town of Dartmouth pointed out that, because they could not vote, they were victims of precisely the same oppression that Britain had tried to impose on its American colonies: taxation without representation.

In December 1780, several of the petitioners were imprisoned for refusing to pay taxes. John Cuffe and his brother Paul continued to protest. They were sons of a Wampanoag Indian woman and an enslaved African American father who managed to purchase himself. Paul Cuffe went on to become a highly successful merchant and shipowner — and to devote a considerable portion of his fortune to the cause of black liberation. His autobiography appears as Document 37.

To the Honourable Council and House of Representatives in General Court Assembled for the State of the Massachusetts Bay in New England.

The petition of several poor Negeros & molattoes who are inhabitants of the Town of Dartmouth, Humbly Sheweth—

That we being chiefly of the African Extract and by Reason of Long Bondag and hard slavery we have been deprived of enjoying the Prophets of our labour or the advantage of inheriting Estates from our parents as our Neighbours the white people do haveing some of us not long enjoyed our own freedom yet of late, contrary to the invariable Custom & Practice of the Country we have been & now are Taxed both in our Polls[1] and that small Pittance of Estate which through

---

[1] *polls*: persons. The poll tax was a "head" or per-person tax.

Massachusetts Division of Archives, Boston.

much hard labour & industry we have got together to sustain ourselves & families withal. We apprehend it therefore to be hard usag[e]
and will doubtless (if Continued will) reduce us to a state of Beggary
whereby we shall become a Burthen to others if not timely prevented
by the Interposition of your justice & power & yor petitioners[2] farther
sheweth, that wee apprehend ourselves to be aggrieved, in that while
we are not allowed the privilege of freemen of the state having no vote
or Influence in the Election of those that Tax us yet many of our colour
(as is well known) have cheerfully Entered the field of Battle in the de-
fence of the common cause and that (as we conceive) against a similar
Exertion of power (in regard to taxation) too well Known to need a
Recital in this place.

Most honourable court we Humbley beseech they would to take
this into consideration and sit us aside from Paying tax or taxes or
cause us to Be Cleared: for we Ever have Been a people that was fair
from all these thing ever since the days of our four fathers and therefore we take it as a heard ship that we should Be so Delt By now in
these difficulty times for there is not to Exceed more then five or six
that hath a cow in this town and theirfore in our Distress we send
unto the thee most Honourable Court for Releaf under the peaceable-
ness of thee people and the mercy of God that we may Be Releaved for
we are not alowed in vooting in the town meating in nor to chuse an
oficer. Neither their was not one Ever heard in the active Court of the
jenerel[3] assembley of us. Wee poor dispised miserable Black people, &
we have not an Eaqual chance with white people Neither By Sea nor
By Land therefore we take it as a heard ship that poor old Negeros
should be Rated[4] which have Been in Bondage some thirty some forty
and some fifty years and now just got their Liberty some by going into
the servicse and some by going to sea and others By good fortan and
also poor distressed mungrels which Have no larning and no land and
also no Work Neither where to put their head But some shelter them
selves into an old rotten hut which thy Dogs would not Lay in. Therefore wee pray that these may give no offense at all By no means But
that thee most Honouerable Court will take it in to consideration as if it
were their own case for we think it as to Be a heard ship that we should
be assessed and not Be a lowed as we may say to Eat Bread therefore

---

[2]*your petitioners*: the signers of this petition.
[3]*jenerel*: general.
[4]*Rated*: taxed.

we Humbley Beg and pray thee to plead our case for us with thy people O god: that those who have the Rule in their hands may Be mercyfull unto the poor and needy give unto those who ask of the and he that would Borrow of thee turn thou not away Empty. O God Be mercyfull unto the Poor and give unto those who giveth ought unto the poor therefore we Return unto thee again: most honouerable Court that thou wouldest Consider us in these difficult times for we send in nor come unto the not with false words Neither with lieing Lips therefore wee think that wee may Be Clear from Being called tories tho some few of our Colour hath rebelled and done Wickedly. How ever we think that their is more of our Collour gone into the wars according to the Number of them in to the Respesicktive towns then any other nation here and here a very therefore We Most Humbley Request therefore that you would take our unhappy case into your serious consideration and in your wisdom and power Grant us Relief from taxation while under our Present depressed Cirsumstances and your poor petioners as in duty bound shall ever pray &c.

Dated at Dartmouth the 10th of February 1780

JOHN CUFFE	his
ADVENTURE CHILDS	PERO + HOWLAND
PAUL CUFFE	mark
his	
SAMUELL + MAY	his
mark	PERO + RUSSELL
	mark
	PERO EGGSHELL

22

WILLIAM CUSHING

Charge to the Jury in the Case of Quok Walker

1783

Through a judicial decree, Massachusetts became the first of the original thirteen states to completely end slavery within its borders. In the early 1780s, several enslaved residents of Massachusetts filed suits contending that slavery violated the state's 1780 constitution, which proclaimed that "all men are born free and equal." One of the plaintiffs was Quok Walker. Nathaniel Jennison, the man who claimed to own Walker, physically assaulted him, and Walker filed criminal charges. In his defense, Jennison contended that he had the right to beat Walker, since Walker was his slave. The chief justice of the Supreme Judicial Court, William Cushing, sided with Walker, instructing the jury to find that Jennison had no right to beat Walker, since the state constitution had abolished slavery. What does Cushing say about the contradictions of slavery?

The jury found Jennison guilty. The effect of this judicial revision and others like it was to end slavery and slaveholding in Massachusetts.

As to the doctrine of slavery and the right of Christians to hold Africans in perpetual servitude, and sell and treat them as we do our horses and cattle, that (it is true) has been heretofore countenanced by the Province Laws formerly, but nowhere is it expressly enacted or established. It has been a usage—a usage which took its origin from the practice of some of the European nations, and the regulations of British government respecting the then Colonies, for the benefit of trade and wealth. But whatever sentiments have formerly prevailed in this particular or slid in upon us by the example of others, a different idea has taken place with the people of America, more favorable to the natural rights of mankind, and to that natural, innate desire of Liberty, with which Heaven (without regard to color, complexion, or shape of

Albert Bushnell Hart, ed., *Commonwealth History of Massachusetts*, 5 vols. (New York: States History Company, 1927–1930), 4:37–38.

noses—features) has inspired all the human race. And upon this ground our Constitution of Government, by which the people of this Commonwealth have solemnly bound themselves, sets out with declaring that all men are born free and equal—and that every subject is entitled to liberty, and to have it guarded by the laws, as well as life and property—and in short is totally repugnant to the idea of being born slaves. This being the case, I think the idea of slavery is inconsistent with our own conduct and Constitution; and there can be no such thing as perpetual servitude of a rational creature, unless his liberty is forfeited by some criminal conduct or given up by personal consent or contract . . . *Verdict Guilty.*

23

SUSAN SEDGWICK

Elizabeth Freeman

1811

Mumbet (later known as Elizabeth Freeman) was born into slavery in New York or western Massachusetts, probably in the 1740s. She fled the Sheffield, Massachusetts, family that claimed ownership of her after the lady of the house struck her with a heated kitchen shovel. In 1781, she persuaded Theodore Sedgwick, a local attorney and prominent politician, to represent her in suing for freedom, which she claimed on the basis of the Massachusetts constitution, which proclaimed that "all men are born free and equal." After winning her case, she changed her name to Elizabeth Freeman and accepted employment as a salaried domestic in the Sedgwick household. In her late sixties, she sat for a miniature portrait by Sedgwick's twenty-three-year-old daughter-in-law, Susan Anne Livingston Ridley Sedgwick. Freeman died on December 28, 1829, and was buried in the Sedgwick family plot in Stockbridge, Massachusetts.

Portrait of Elizabeth "Mumbet" Freeman (c. 1742–1829) (w/c on ivory) by Susan Anne Livingston Ridley Sedgwick (fl. 1811). © Massachusetts Historical Society, Boston/The Bridgeman Art Library.

24

JOHN MARRANT

A Narrative of the Lord's Wonderful Dealings with John Marrant, a Black

July 18, 1785

Born free in New York City on June 15, 1755, and converted to evangelical Christianity at the age of thirteen by the traveling minister George Whitefield, John Marrant spent part of his teenage years in a village of Cherokee Indians. During the Revolutionary War, he served in the British navy. He settled in London after the war but then traveled to Nova Scotia in 1785 as a Methodist missionary, focusing his efforts both on black Loyalist refugees and on the Mi'kmaq Indians. Lack of financial support forced him to leave Nova Scotia. He went first to Boston and later to London, where he died on April 15, 1791, at the age of thirty-five. Throughout his career, Marrant faced harassment from whites who did not approve of the idea of a popular black minister.

I JOHN MARRANT, born June 15th, 1755, in New-York, in North-America, wish these gracious dealings of the Lord with me to be published, in hopes they may be useful to others, to encourage the fearful, to confirm the wavering, and to refresh the hearts of true believers. My father died when I was little more than four years of age, and before I was five my mother removed from New-York to St. Augustine, about seven hundred miles from that city. Here I was sent to school, and taught to read and spell; after we had resided here about eighteen months, it was found necessary to remove to Georgia, where we remained; and I was kept to school until I had attained my eleventh year. The Lord spoke to me in my early days, by these removes, if I could have understood him, and said, "Here we have no continuing city."

We left Georgia, and went to Charles-Town,[1] where it was intended I should be put apprentice to some trade. Some time after I had been

---

[1] *Charles-Town*: Charleston, South Carolina.

John Marrant, *A Narrative of the Lord's Wonderful Dealings with John Marrant, a Black*, 2nd ed. (London: Gilbert and Plummer, 1785), 7–11, 21–24, 29–38.

in Charles-Town, as I was walking one day, I passed by a school, and heard music and dancing, which took my fancy very much, and I felt a strong inclination to learn the music. I went home, and informed my sister, that I had rather learn to play upon music than go to a trade.[2] She told me she could do nothing in it, until she had acquainted my mother with my desire. Accordingly she wrote a letter upon it to my mother, which, when she read, the contents were disapproved of by her, and she came to Charles-Town to prevent it. She persuaded me much against it, but her persuasions were fruitless. Disobedience either to God or man, being one of the fruits of sin, grew out from me in early buds. Finding I was set upon it, and resolved to learn nothing else, she agreed to it, and went with me to speak to the man, and to settle upon the best terms with him she could. He insisted upon twenty pounds down, which was paid, and I was engaged to stay with him eighteen months, and my mother to find me every thing during that term. The first day I went to him he put the violin into my hand, which pleased me much, and, applying close, I learned very fast, not only to play, but to dance also; so that in six months I was able to play for the whole school.

In the evenings after the scholars were dismissed, I used to resort to the bottom of our garden, where it was customary for some musicians to assemble to blow the French-horn. Here my improvement was so rapid, that in a twelve-month's time I became master both of the violin and of the French horn, and was much respected by the Gentlemen and Ladies whose children attended the school, as also by my master: This opened to me a large door of vanity and vice, for I was invited to all the balls and assemblies that were held in the town, and met with the general applause of the inhabitants. I was a stranger to want, being supplied with as much money as I had any occasion for; which my sister observing, said, "You have now no need of a trade." I was now in my thirteenth year, devoted to pleasure and drinking in iniquity like water; a slave to every vice suited to my nature and to my years. The time I had engaged to serve my master being expired, he persuaded me to stay with him, and offered me any thing, or any money, not to leave him. His intreaties proving ineffectual, I quitted his service, and visited my mother in the country; with her I staid two months, living without God or hope in the world, fishing and hunting on the sabbath-day. Unstable as water I returned to town, and wished to go to some trade. My sister's husband being informed of

---

[2]*go to a trade:* learn a useful skill.

my inclination provided me with a master, on condition that I should serve him one year and a half on trial, and afterwards be bound, if he approved of me.

Accordingly I went, but every evening I was sent for to play on music, somewhere or another; and I often continued out very late, sometimes all night, so as to render me incapable of attending my master's business the next day; yet in this manner I served him a year and four months, and was much approved of by him. He wrote a letter to my mother to come and have me bound, and whilst my mother was weighing the matter in her own mind, the gracious purposes of God, respecting a perishing sinner, were now to be disclosed. One evening I was sent for in a very particular manner to go and play for some Gentlemen, which I agreed to do, and was on my way to fulfil my promise; and passing by a large meeting house I saw many lights in it, and crouds of people going in. I enquired what it meant, and was answered by my companion, that a crazy man was hallooing there; this raised my curiosity to go in, that I might hear what he was hallooing about. He persuaded me not to go in, but in vain. He then said, "If you will do one thing I will go in with you." I asked him what that was? He replied, "Blow the French-horn among them." I liked the proposal well enough, but expressed my fears of being beaten for disturbing them; but upon his promising to stand by and defend me, I agreed.

So we went, and with much difficulty got within the doors. I was pushing the people to make room, to get the horn off my shoulder to blow it, just as Mr. Whitefield[3] was naming his text, and looking round, and, as I thought, directly upon me, and pointing with his finger, he uttered these words, "PREPARE TO MEET THY GOD, O ISRAEL." The Lord accompanied the word with such power, that I was struck to the ground, and lay both speechless and senseless for twenty four minutes. When I was come a little too, I found two men attending me, and a woman throwing water in my face, and holding a smelling-bottle to my nose; and when something more recovered, every word I heard from the minister was like a parcel of swords thrust into me, and what added to my distress, I thought I saw the devil on every side of me. I was constrained in the bitterness of my spirit to halloo out in the midst of the congregation, which disturbing them, they took me away; but finding I could neither walk or stand, they carried me as far as the vestry, and there I remained till the service was over. When the

---

[3]*Mr. Whitefield*: Rev. George Whitefield (1714–1770), the most prominent leader of a religious revival known in America as the Great Awakening.

people were dismissed Mr. Whitefield came into the vestry, and being told of my condition he came immediately, and the first word he said to me was, "JESUS CHRIST HAS GOT THEE AT LAST." . . .

[Marrant then wandered into the woods on a religious quest that lasted several weeks, and he was befriended by an Indian hunter.]

The hunting season being now at an end, we left the woods, and directed our course towards a large Indian town, belonging to the Cherokee nation; and having reached it, I said to the hunter, they will not suffer me to enter in. He replied, as I was with him, nobody would interrupt me.

There was an Indian fortification all round the town, and a guard placed at each entrance. The hunter passed one of these without molestation, but I was stopped by the guard and examined. They asked me where I came from, and what was my business there? My companion of the woods attempted to speak for me, but was not permitted; he was taken away, and I saw him no more. I was now surrounded by about 50 men, and carried to one of their chiefs to be examined by him. When I came before him, he asked me what was my business there? I told him I came there with a hunter, whom I met with in the woods. He replied, "Did I not know that whoever came there without giving a better account of themselves than I did, was to be put to death?" I said I did not know it. Observing that I answered him so readily in his own language, he asked me where I learnt it? To this I returned no answer, but burst out into a flood of tears, and calling upon my Lord Jesus.

At this he stood astonished, and expressed a concern for me, and said I was young. He asked me who my Lord Jesus was?—To this I gave him no answer, but continued praying and weeping. Addressing himself to the officer who stood by him, he said he was sorry; but it was the law, and it must not be broken. I was then ordered to be taken away, and put into a place of confinement. They led me from their court into a low dark place, and thrust me into it, very dreary and dismal; they made fast the door, and set a watch. The judge sent for the executioner, and gave him his warrant for my execution in the afternoon of the next day. The executioner came, and gave me notice of it, which made me very happy, as the near prospect of death made me hope for a speedy deliverance from the body: And truly this dungeon became my chapel, for the Lord Jesus did not leave me in this great trouble, but was very present, so that I continued blessing him, and singing his praises all night without ceasing: The watch hearing the noise, informed the executioner that somebody had been in the dungeon with me all night; upon which he came in to see and to examine, with a great torch lighted in his hand, who it was I had with me; but finding nobody, he turned round, and asked me who it was? and I told him it was the Lord Jesus Christ; but he made no answer, turned away, went out, and locked the door. At the hour appointed for my execution I was taken out, and led to the destined spot, amidst a vast number of people. I praised the Lord all the way we went, and when we arrived at the place I understood the kind of death I was to suffer, yet, blessed be God, none of those things moved me. The executioner shewed me a basket of turpentine wood, stuck full of small pieces, like skewers; he told me I was to be stripped naked, and laid down in the basket, and these sharp pegs were to be stuck into me, and then set on fire, and when they had burnt to my body, I was to be turned on the other side, and served in the same manner, and then to be taken by four men and thrown into the flame, which was to finish the execution. I burst into tears, and asked what I had done to deserve so cruel a death! To this he gave me no answer. I cried out, Lord, if it be thy will that it should be so, thy will be done: I then asked the executioner to let me go to prayer; he asked me to whom? I answered, to the Lord my God; he seemed surprized, and asked me where he was? I told him he was present; upon which he gave me leave. I desired them all to do as I did, so I fell down upon my knees, and mentioned to the Lord his delivering of the three children in the fiery furnace, and of Daniel in the lion's den, and had close communion with God. I prayed in English a considerable time, and about the middle of my prayer, the Lord impressed a strong desire upon my mind to turn into their language, and pray in their tongue. I did so, and with remarkable liberty, which wonderfully affected the people. One circumstance was very singular, and strikingly displays the power and grace of God. I believe the executioner was savingly converted to God. He rose from his knees, and embraced me round the middle, and was unable to speak for about five minutes; the first words he expressed, when he had utterance, were, "No man shall hurt thee. . . ."

I began now to feel an inclination growing upon me to go farther on, but none to return home. The king being acquainted with this, expressed his fears of my being used ill by the next Indian nation, and, to prevent it, sent 50 men, and a recommendation to the king, with me. The next nation was called the Creek Indians, at 60 miles distance. Here I was received with kindness, owing to the king's influence, from whom I had parted; here I staid five weeks. I next visited the Catawar Indians, at about 55 miles distance from the others:

Lastly, I went among the Housaw Indians, 80 miles distant from the last mentioned; here I staid seven weeks. These nations were then at peace with each other, and I passed among them without danger, being recommended from one to the other. When they recollect, that the white people drove them from the American shores, the three first nations have often united, and murdered all the white people in the back settlements which they could lay hold of, man, woman, and child. I had not much reason to believe any of these three nations were savingly wrought upon, and therefore I returned to the Cherokee nation, which took me up eight weeks. I continued with my old friends seven weeks and two days.

I now and then found, that my affections to my family and country were not dead; they were sometimes very sensibly felt, and at last strengthened into an invincible desire of returning home. The king was much against it; but feeling the same strong bias towards my country, after we had asked Divine direction, the king consented, and accompanied me 60 miles with 140 men. I went to prayer three times before we could part, and then he sent 40 men with me a hundred miles farther; I went to prayer, and then took my leave of them, and passed on my way. I had 70 miles now to go to the back settlements of the white people. I was surrounded very soon with wolves again, which made my old lodging [up in trees] both necessary and welcome. However it was not long, for in two days I reached the settlements, and on the third I found a house: It was about dinner-time, and as I came up to the door the family saw me, were frightened, and ran away. I sat down to dinner alone, and eat very heartily, and, after returning God thanks, I went to see what was become of the family. I found means to lay hold of a girl that stood peeping at me from behind a barn. She fainted away, and it was upwards of an hour before she recovered; it was nine o'clock before I could get them all to venture in, they were so terrified.

My dress was purely in the Indian stile; the skins of wild beasts composed my garments, my head was set out in the savage manner, with a long pendant down my back, a sash round my middle without breeches, and a tomohawk by my side. In about two days they became sociable. Having visited three or four other families, at the distance of 16 or 20 miles, I got them altogether to prayer on the Sabbath days, to the number of 17 persons. I staid with them six weeks, and they expressed much sorrow when I left them. I was now one hundred and twelve miles from home. On the road I sometimes met with a house, then I was hospitably entertained; and when I met with none, a tree lent me the use of its friendly shelter and protection from the prowling beasts of the woods during the night. The God of mercy and grace supported me thus for eight days, and on the ninth I reached my uncle's house.

The following particulars, relating to the manner in which I was made known to my family, are less interesting; and yet, perhaps, some readers would not forgive their omission: I shall, however, be as brief as I can. I asked my uncle for a lodging, which he refused. I enquired how far the town was off; three quarters of a mile, said he. Do you know Mrs. Marrant and family, and how the children do? was my next question. He said he did, they were all well, but one was lately lost; at this I turned my head and wept. He did not know me, and upon refusing again to lodge me, I departed. When I reached the town it was dark, and passing by a house where one of my old school-fellows lived, I knocked at the door; he came out, and asked me what I wanted? I desired a lodging, which was granted: I went in, but was not known. I asked him if he knew Mrs. Marrant, and how the family were? He said, he had just left them, they were all well; but a young lad, with whom he went to school, who, after he had quitted school, went to Charles-Town to learn some trade; but came home crazy, and rambled in the woods, and was torn in pieces by the wild beasts. How do you know, said I, that he was killed by wild beasts? I, and his brother, and uncle, and others, said he, went three days into the woods in search of him, and found his carcase torn, and brought it home, and buried it, and are now in mourning for him. This affected me very much, and I wept; observing it, he said, what is the matter? I made no answer. At supper they sat down without craving a blessing, for which I reproved them; this so affected the man, that I believe it ended in a sound conversion. Here is a wild man, says he, come out of the woods to be a witness for God, and to reprove our ingratitude and stupefaction! After supper I went to prayer, and then to bed. Rising a little before day-light, and praising the Lord, as my custom was, the family were surprised, and got up: I staid with them till nine o'clock, and then went to my mother's house in the next street. The singularity of my dress drew every body's eyes upon me, yet none knew me. I knock'd at my mother's door, my sister opened it, and was startled at my appearance. Having expressed a desire to see Mrs. Marrant, I was answered, she was not very well, and that my business with her could be done by the person at the door, who also attempted to shut me out, which I prevented. My mother being called, I went in, and sat down, a mob of people being round the door. My mother asked, "what is your business;" only to see you, said I. She was much obliged to me, but did not know me. I asked, how are your children? how are your two sons? She replied, her daughters were in good health, of her two sons, one was well, and with her, but the other,—unable to contain, she burst into a flood of tears, and retired. I was overcome, and wept much; but nobody knew me. This was an affecting scene! Presently my brother came in: He enquired, who I was, and what I was? My sister did not know; but being uneasy at my presence, they contrived to get me out of the house, which, being over-heard by me, I resolved not to stir. My youngest sister, eleven years of age, came in from school, and knew me the moment she saw me: She goes into the kitchen, and tells the woman her brother was come; but her news finding no credit there she returns, passes through the room where I sat, made a running curtsey, and says to my eldest sister in the next room, it is my brother! She was then called a foolish girl, and threatened; the child cried, and insisted upon it. She went crying up-stairs to my mother, and told her; but neither would my mother believe her. At last they said to her, if it be your brother, go and kiss him, and ask him how he does? She ran and clasped me round the neck, and, looking me in the face, said, "Are not you my brother John?" I answered yes, and wept. I was then made known to all the family, to my friends, and acquaintances, who received me, and were glad, and rejoiced: Thus the dead was brought to life again; thus the lost was found. I shall now close the Narrative, with only remarking a few incidents in my life, until my connection with my Right Honourable Patroness, the Countess of HUNTINGDON.

I remained with my relations till the commencement of the American troubles. I used to go and hear the word of God, if any Gospel ministers came into the country, though at a considerable distance; and yet, reader, my soul was got into a declining state. Don't forget our Lord's exhortation, "What I say unto you, I say unto all, WATCH."

In those troublesome times, I was pressed on board the Scorpion sloop of war, as their musician, as they were told I could play on music. I continued in his majesty's service six years and eleven months; and with shame confess, that a lamentable stupor crept over all my spiritual vivacity, life and vigour; I got cold and dead. My gracious God, my dear Father in his dear Son, roused me every now and then by dangers and deliverances.—I was at the siege of Charles-Town, and passed through many dangers. When the town was taken, my old royal benefactor and convert, the king of the Cherokee Indians, riding into the town with general Clinton, saw me, and knew me: He alighted off his horse, and came to me; said he was glad to see me; that his daughter was very happy, and sometimes longed to get out of the body.

Some time after this I was cruising about in the American seas, and cannot help mentioning a singular deliverance I had from the most imminent danger, and the use the Lord made of it to me. We were overtaken by a violent storm; I was washed overboard, and thrown on again; dashed into the sea a second time, and tossed upon deck again. I now fastened a rope round my middle, as a security against being thrown into the sea again; but, alas! forgot to fasten it to any part of the ship; being carried away the third time by the fury of the waves, when in the sea, I found the rope both useless and an incumbrance. I was in the sea the third time about eight minutes, and the sharks came round me in great numbers; one of an enormous size, that could easily have taken me into his mouth at once, passed and rubbed against my side. I then cried more earnestly to the Lord than I had done for some time; and he who heard Jonah's prayer, did not shut out mine, for I was thrown aboard again; these were the means the Lord used to revive me, and I began now to set out afresh.

I was in the engagement with the Dutch off the Dogger Bank, on board the Princess-Amelia, of 84 guns. We had a great number killed and wounded; the deck was running with blood; six men were killed, and three wounded, stationed at the same gun with me; my head and face were covered with the blood and brains of the slain: I was wounded, but did not fall, till a quarter of an hour before the engagement ended, and was happy during the whole of it. After being in the hospital three months and 16 days, I was sent to the West-Indies on board a ship of war, and, after cruising in those seas, we returned home as a convoy. Being taken ill of my old wounds, I was put into the hospital at Plymouth, and had not been there long, when the physician gave it as his opinion, that I should not be capable of serving the king again; I was therefore discharged, and came to London, where I lived with a respectable and pious merchant three years, who was unwilling to part with me. During this time I saw my call to the ministry fuller and clearer; had a feeling concern for the salvation of my countrymen: I carried them constantly in the arms of prayer and faith to the throne of grace, and had continual sorrow in my heart for my brethren, for my kinsmen, according to the flesh.—I wrote a letter to my brother, who returned me an answer, in which he prayed some ministers would come and preach to them, and desired me to shew it to the minister whom I attended. I used to exercise my gifts on a Monday evening in prayer and exhortation, and was approved of, and ordained at Bath. Her Ladyship having seen the letter from my brother in Nova-Scotia, thought Providence called me there: To which place I am now bound, and expect to sail in a few days.

I have now only to intreat the earnest prayers of all my kind Christian friends, that I may be carried safe there; kept humble, made faithful, and successful; that strangers may hear of and run to Christ; that Indian tribes may stretch out their hands to God; that the black nations may be made white in the blood of the Lamb; that vast multitudes of hard tongues, and of a strange speech, may learn the language of Canaan, and sing the song of Moses, and of the Lamb; and, anticipating the glorious prospect, may we all with fervent hearts, and willing tongues, sing hallelujah; the kingdoms of the world are become the kingdoms of our God, and of his Christ. Amen and Amen.

London,
Prescot-street, No. 60,
July 18, 1785.

25

CITIZENS OF HALIFAX COUNTY

Petition to the Virginia
General Assembly
November 10, 1785

This petition, presented to the Virginia legislature three years after the passage of legislation that allowed slaveholders to manumit their slaves, reveals the fears of some white citizens. During 1784 and 1785, more than a thousand white Virginians signed petitions defending slavery. On what basis did they make their claims?

Virginia Legislative Petitions, Halifax County, Box 91, Folder 21, Library of Virginia, Richmond.

To the honourable the General Assembly of Virginia the Remonstrance and Petition of the Free Inhabitants of Halifax County.

Gentlemen,

When the British Parliament usurped a Right to dispose of our Property[1] without our Consent, we dissolved the Union with our Parent Country, & established a Constitution and Form of Government of our own, that our Property might be secure in Future. In Order to effect this, we risked our Lives & Fortunes, and waded through Seas of Blood. Divine Providence smiled on our Enterprize, and crowned it with Success. And our Rights of Liberty and Property are now as well secured to us, as they can be by any human Constitution & Form of Government.

But notwithstanding this, we understand, a very subtle and daring Attempt is on Foot to deprive us of a very important Part of our Property. An Attempt carried on by the Enemies of our Country, Tools of the British Administration, and supported by a Number of deluded Men among us, to wrest from us our Slaves by an Act of the Legislature for a general Emancipation of them. They have the Address,[2] indeed to cover their Design, with the Veil of Piety and Liberality of Sentiment. But it is unsupported by the Word of God, and will be ruinous to Individuals and to the Public.

It is unsupported by the Word of God. Under the Old Testament Dispensation, Slavery was permitted by the Deity himself. Thus it is recorded, Levit.[3] Chap. 25. Ver. 44, 45, 46. "Both thy Bond-men, and Bond-maids, which thou shalt have, shall be of the Heathen that are round about you; of them shall ye buy Bond-men and Bond-maids. Moreover, of the Children of the Strangers, that do sojourn among you of them shall ye buy, and of their Families that are with you, which they beget in your Land, and they shall be your Possession, and ye shall take them, as an Inheritance for your Children after you, to inherit them for a Possession; they shall be your Bond-men forever." This Permission to possess and inherit Bond Servants, we have Reason to conclude, was continued through all the Revolutions of[4] the Jewish Government, down to the Advent of our Lord. And we do not find, that either he or his Apostles abridged it. On the Contrary, the

---

[1] *dispose of our Property*: spend our money.
[2] *Address*: cleverness.
[3] *Levit*: Leviticus.
[4] *Revolutions of*: changes in.

Freedom which the Followers of Jesus were taught to expect, was a Freedom from the Bondage of Sin and Satan, and from the Dominion of their Lusts and Passions; but as to their outward Condition, whatever that was, whether Bond or Free, when they embraced Christianity, it was to remain the same afterwards. This Saint Paul hath expressly told us 1 Cor.[5] Chap. 7. Ver. 20th. where he is speaking directly to this very Point; "Let every Man abide in the same Calling, wherein he is called;" and at Ver. 24. "Let every Man wherein he is called therein abide with God." Thus it is evident the above Attempt is unsupported by the Divine Word.

It is also ruinous to Individuals & to the Public.[6] For it involves in it, and is productive of Want, Poverty, Distress, and Ruin to the Free Citizen; Neglect, Famine, and Death to the helpless black Infant & superannuated[7] Parent; the Horrors of all the Rapes, Murders, and Outrages, which a vast Multitude of unprincipled, unpropertied, vindictive, and remorseless Banditti are capable of perpetrating; inevitable Bankruptcy to the Revenue,[8] and consequently Breach of public Faith, and Loss of Credit with foreign Nations; and lastly Ruin to this now free and flourishing Country.

We therefore your Remonstrants and Petitioners do solemnly adjure and humbly pray you, that you will discountenance and utterly reject every Motion and Proposal for emancipating our Slaves; that as the Act lately made, empowering the Owners of Slaves to liberate them, has been and is still productive, in some Measure, of sundry of the above pernicious Effects, you will immediately and totally repeal it; and that as many of the Slaves, liberated by the said Act, have been guilty of Thefts and Outrages, Insolences and Violences destructive to the Peace, Safety, and Happiness of Society, you will make effectual Provision for the due Government of them.

And your Remonstrants & Petitioners shall ever pray, &c.

---

[5] *Cor.*: Corinthians.
[6] *Public*: government.
[7] *superannuated*: old.
[8] *the Revenue*: the state budget.

26

PRINCE HALL AND OTHER FREE BLACKS

Petition to the Massachusetts Legislature
January 4, 1787

Throughout U.S. history, some African Americans, having given up on ever being treated equally in the United States, have left the country, often resettling in Africa. One of the first proposals for mass emigration was put forward by the African American Masonic lodge in Boston, whose Grand Master was Prince Hall. Born into slavery in Bridgetown, Barbados, in the 1730s or 1740s, Hall was the son of an Englishman and a woman of African and French descent. He somehow found his way to Boston, where he was manumitted in 1770. Hall and his fellow masons asked the Massachusetts legislature to provide financial support for their resettlement plan. The petition was denied, but several privately funded expeditions were launched.

To the honourable, the general Court of the Commonwealth of the Massachusetts Bay The petition of the subscribers, a number of African Blacks, humbly sheweth.

That we, or our ancestors have been taken from all our dear connections, and brought from Africa and put into a state of slavery in this country; from which unhappy situation we have been lately in some measure delivered by the new constitution which has been adopted by this state, or by the free act of our former masters. But we yet find ourselves, in many respects, in very disagreable and disadvantageous circumstances; most of which must attend us, so long as we and our children live in America.

This, and other considerations which we need not here particularly mention, induce us earnestly to desire to return to Africa, our native country, which warm climate is much more natural and agreable to us; and, for which the God of nature has formed us; and, where we shall live among our equals, and be more comfortable and happy, than

Massachusetts Division of Archives, Boston.

we can be in our present situation; and, at the same time, may have a prospect of usefulness to our brethren there.

This leads us humbly to propose the following plan to the consideration of this honourable Court. The soil of our native country is good, and produces the necessaries of life in great abundance. There are large tracts of uncultivated lands, which, if proper application were made for them, it is presumed, might be obtained, and would be freely given for those to settle upon, who shall be disposed to return to them. When this shall be effected by a number of Blacks, sent there for this purpose, who shall be thought most capable of making such an application, and transacting this business; then they who are disposed to go and settle there shall form themselves into a civil society, united by a political constitution, in which they shall agree: And those who are disposed, and shall be thought qualified, shall unite, and be formed into a religious society, or christian church; and have one or more blacks ordained as their pastors or Bishops: And being thus formed, shall remove to Africa, and settle on said lands.

These must be furnished with necessary provisions for the voyage; and with farming utensils necessary to cultivate the land; and with the materials which cannot at present be obtained there, and which will be needed to build houses and mills.

The execution of this plan will, we hope, be the means of inlightening and civilizing those nations, who are now sunk in ignorance and barbarity; and may give opportunity to those who shall be disposed, and engaged to promote the salvation of their heathen brethren, to spread the knowledge of Christianity among them, and persuade them to embrace it. And schools may be formed to instruct their youth and children, and christian knowledge be spread through many nations who now are in gross darkness; and christian churches be formed, and the only true God and Saviour be worshiped and honoured through that vast extent of country, where are now the habitations of cruelty under the reign of the prince of darkness.

This may also lay a happy foundation for a friendly and lasting connection between that country and the United States of America, by a mutual intercourse and profitable commerce, which may much more than overbalance all the expence which is now necessary in order to carry this plan into effect.

This leads us to observe, that we are poor and utterly unable to prosecute this scheme or to return to Africa, without assistance. Money is wanted to enable those who shall be appointed, to go to Africa, and procure lands to settle upon; and to obtain a passage for us and our families; and to furnish us with the necessary provisions, and the utensils and articles that have been mentioned.

We therefore humbly and earnestly apply to this honourable Court, hoping and praying that in your wisdom and goodness, you concert and prosecute the best method to relieve and assist us, either by granting a brief for a collection in all the congregations in this State, or in any other way, which shall to your wisdom appear most expedient. And your petitioners shall, as in duty bound, always pray.

27

ABSALOM JONES, RICHARD ALLEN, AND OTHERS

Charter of the Free African Society

April 12, 1787

Nearly all of the thousands of African Americans who obtained their freedom during the Revolutionary era faced continuing hardship. Most white people harbored strong prejudices against them, and most free blacks were continuously subjected to discrimination, exploitation, and abuse. One way African Americans coped with these harsh conditions was by banding together to form a wide variety of civic and religious organizations. For nearly all of them, a primary mission was mutual aid. In Philadelphia, two ministers, Absalom Jones and Richard Allen, took the lead in forming the Free African Society.

We, the free Africans and their descendants, of the City of Philadelphia, in the State of Pennsylvania, or elsewhere, do unanimously agree, for the benefit of each other, to advance one shilling in silver Pennsylvania currency a month; and after one year's subscription from the date hereof, then to hand forth to the needy of this Society, if any should require, the sum of three shillings and nine pence per week of the said money: provided, this necessity is not brought on them by their own imprudence.

William Douglass, *Annals of the First African Church in the United States of America, Now Styled the African Episcopal Church of St. Thomas, Philadelphia* . . . (Philadelphia: King & Baird, 1862), 15–17.

And it is further agreed, that no drunkard nor disorderly person be admitted as a member, and if any should prove disorderly after having been received, the said disorderly person shall be disjointed from us if there is not an amendment, by being informed by two of the members, without having any of his subscription money returned.

And if any should neglect paying his monthly subscription for three months, and after having been informed of the same by two of the members, and no sufficient reason appearing for such neglect, if he do not pay the whole the next ensuing meeting, he shall be disjointed from us, by being informed by two of the members as an offender, without having any of his subscription money returned.

Also, if any person neglect meeting every month, for every omission he shall pay three pence, except in case of sickness or any other complaint that should require the assistance of the Society, then, and in such a case, he shall be exempt from the fines and subscription during the said sickness.

Also, we apprehend it to be just and reasonable, that the surviving widow of a deceased member should enjoy the benefit of this Society so long as she remains his widow, complying with the rules thereof, excepting the subscriptions.

And we apprehend it to be necessary, that the children of our deceased members be under the care of the Society, so far as to pay for the education of their children, if they cannot attend the free school; also to put them out apprentices to suitable trades or places, if required.

Also, that no member shall convene the Society together; but, it shall be the sole business of the committee, and that only on special occasions, and to dispose of the money in hand to the best advantage for the use of the Society, after they are granted the liberty at a monthly meeting, and to transact all other business whatsoever, except that of Clerk and Treasurer.

And we unanimously agree to choose Joseph Clarke to be our Clerk and Treasurer; and whenever another should succeed him, it is always understood, that one of the people called Quakers, belonging to one of the three monthly meetings in Philadelphia, is to be chosen to act as Clerk and Treasurer of this useful Institution.

The following persons met, viz., Absalom Jones, Richard Allen, Samuel Baston, Joseph Johnson, Cato Freeman, Caesar Cranchell, and James Potter, also William White, whose early assistance and useful remarks we found truly profitable. This evening the articles were read, and after some beneficial remarks were made, they were agreed unto.

RAPHAELLE PEALE

Absalom Jones

1810

Absalom Jones was born into slavery in Delaware in 1746. At the age of sixteen, he was separated from his family and transported to Philadelphia. Working a variety of odd jobs, he earned enough to purchase his wife's freedom and then, in 1784, his own. The Joneses worshipped at Philadelphia's racially integrated St. George's Methodist Church until the church's white majority decided to compel black members to sit in the balcony. When Jones defied the new policy, a group of white men tried to make him move, whereupon he and the other black members of the church staged a walkout. Later, Jones helped found St. Thomas Episcopal Church—the first black Episcopal church in the United States—and became its pastor. He died in 1818.

In 1810 Raphaelle Peale (1794–1825), of the prominent family of artists, painted this portrait of Absalom Jones. Notice Jones's clerical collar.

29

Rose Fortune

1780s?

Of the thousands of African Americans who freed themselves during the Revolutionary War by casting their lots with the British, more than half were women and children. Among them was a young girl who took the name Rose Fortune. Resettled in the town of Annapolis Royal in Nova Scotia, a British colony that had remained loyal to the crown, Fortune supported herself by transporting luggage and provisions from ships that docked in the town's harbor. Reportedly born in Virginia in the 1770s, Fortune died in February 1864 at the age of about ninety. This watercolor is by an unknown artist.

Rose Fortune (ca. 1774–1864), anonymous artist, 1830s? Nova Scotia Archives Documentary Art Collection (Halifax, NS), 1979-147/56 (N-6955; CN-9813).

30

CAPTAIN WILLIAM BOOTH

A Black Wood Cutter at Shelburne, Nova Scotia

1788

The black Loyalists who resettled in Nova Scotia found whatever employment they could. Many were able to resume the occupations they had practiced as slaves, which may have been the case with the anonymous woodcutter depicted in this watercolor by William Booth, a captain in the British army's Corps of Engineers.

31

THOMAS JEFFERSON

Notes on the State of Virginia

1788

The sole book published by Thomas Jefferson was called Notes on the State of Virginia. *The project began when a Frenchman who was writing an encyclopedia sent Jefferson, then governor of Virginia, a list of questions about the state. Jefferson wrote out a long series of answers that he eventually expanded into a full-length book. In one section, he lists laws he hopes the state legislature will someday pass. One would emancipate Virginia's slaves and send them to "other parts of the world." Jefferson goes on to explain why he believes the emancipated slaves cannot be incorporated into Virginia society. How can you reconcile these opinions with Jefferson's original draft of the Declaration of Independence? What effect does Jefferson think slavery has on slaveholders and the American Republic?*

To emancipate all slaves born after passing the act. The bill reported by the revisors[1] does not itself contain this proposition;[2] but an amendment containing it was prepared, to be offered to the legislature whenever the bill should be taken up, and further directing, that they should continue with their parents to a certain age, then be brought up, at the public expence, to tillage,[3] arts or sciences, according to their geniusses,[4] till the females should be eighteen, and the males twenty-one years of age, when they should be colonized to such place as the circumstances of the time should render most proper, sending them out with arms, implements of houshold and of the handicraft arts, seeds, pairs of the useful domestic animals, &c. to declare them a

---

[1] *the revisors*: committee appointed by the Virginia legislature to update the laws of the newly independent state.
[2] *this proposition*: the proposal to free the slaves.
[3] *tillage*: farming.
[4] *geniusses*: abilities.

From Thomas Jefferson, *Notes on the State of Virginia* (Philadelphia: Prichard and Hall, 1788), 146–50, 154, 172–74.

free and independant people, and extend to them our alliance and protection, till they have acquired strength; and to send vessels at the same time to other parts of the world for an equal number of white inhabitants; to induce whom to migrate hither, proper encouragements were to be proposed. It will probably be asked, Why not retain and incorporate the blacks into the state, and thus save the expence of supplying, by importation of white settlers, the vacancies they will leave? Deep rooted prejudices entertained by the whites; ten thousand recollections, by the blacks, of the injuries they have sustained; new provocations; the real distinctions which nature has made; and many other circumstances, will divide us into parties, and produce convulsions which will probably never end but in the extermination of the one or the other race.—To these objections, which are political, may be added others, which are physical and moral. The first difference which strikes us is that of colour. Whether the black of the negro resides in the reticular membrane between the skin and scarf-skin, or in the scarf-skin itself; whether it proceeds from the colour of the blood, the colour of the bile, or from that of some other secretion, the difference is fixed in nature, and is as real as if its seat and cause were better known to us. And is this difference of no importance? Is it not the foundation of a greater or less share of beauty in the two races? Are not the fine mixtures of red and white, the expressions of every passion by greater or less suffusions of colour in the one, preferable to that eternal monotony, which reigns in the countenances, that immoveable veil of black which covers all the emotions of the other race? Add to these, flowing hair, a more elegant symmetry of form, their own judgment in favour of the whites, declared by their preference of them, as uniformly as is the preference of the Oranootan[5] for the black women over those of his own species. The circumstance of superior beauty, is thought worthy attention in the propagation of our horses, dogs, and other domestic animals; why not in that of man? Besides those of colour, figure, and hair, there are other physical distinctions proving a difference of race. They have less hair on the face and body. They secrete less by the kidnies, and more by the glands of the skin, which gives them a very strong and disagreeable odour. This greater degree of transpiration[6] renders them more tolerant of heat, and less so of cold, than the whites. Perhaps too a difference of structure in the pulmonary apparatus,[7] which a late ingenious experimentalist

[5] *Oranootan*: orangutan.
[6] *transpiration*: sweat.
[7] *pulmonary apparatus*: lungs.

has discovered to be the principal regulator of animal heat, may have disabled them from extricating, in the act of inspiration,[8] so much of that fluid from the outer air, or obliged them in expiration, to part with more of it. They seem to require less sleep. A black after hard labour through the day, will be induced by the slightest amusements to sit up till midnight, or later, though knowing he must be out with the first dawn of the morning. They are at least as brave, and more adventuresome. But this may perhaps proceed from a want of fore-thought, which prevents their seeing a danger till it be present. When present, they do not go through it with more coolness or steadiness than the whites. They are more ardent[9] after their female: but love seems with them to be more an eager desire, than a tender delicate mixture of sentiment and sensation. Their griefs are transient.[10] Those numberless afflictions, which render it doubtful whether heaven has given life to us in mercy or in wrath, are less felt, and sooner forgotten with them. In general, their existence appears to participate more of sensation than reflection. To this must be ascribed their disposition to sleep when abstracted from their diversions, and unemployed in labour. An animal whose body is at rest, and who does not reflect, must be disposed to sleep of course. Comparing them by their faculties of memory, reason, and imagination, it appears to me, that in memory they are equal to the whites; in reason much inferior, as I think one could scarcely be found capable of tracing and comprehending the investigations of Euclid;[11] and that in imagination they are dull, tasteless, and anomalous. It would be unfair to follow them to Africa for this investigation. We will consider them here, on the same stage with the whites, and where the facts are not apocryphal[12] on which a judgment is to be formed. It will be right to make great allowances for the difference of condition, of education, of conversation, of the sphere in which they move. Many millions of them have been brought to, and born in America. Most of them indeed have been confined to tillage, to their own homes, and their own society: yet many have been so situated, that they might have availed themselves of the conversation of their masters; many have been brought up to the handicraft arts,[13] from that circumstance have always been associated with the whites. Some

[8]*inspiration*: breathing.
[9]*ardent*: lustful.
[10]*transient*: short-lived.
[11]*Euclid*: famous Greek geometer.
[12]*apocryphal*: legendary.
[13]*handicraft arts*: craft skills such as carpentry and shoemaking.

have been liberally educated, and all have lived in countries where the arts and sciences are cultivated to a considerable degree, and have had before their eyes samples of the best works from abroad. The Indians, with no advantages of this kind, will often carve figures on their pipes not destitute of design and merit. They will crayon out an animal, a plant, or a country, so as to prove the existence of a germ in their minds which only wants[14] cultivation. They astonish you with strokes of the most sublime oratory; such as prove their reason and sentiment strong, their imagination glowing and elevated. But never yet could I find that a black had uttered a thought above the level of plain narration; never see even an elementary trait of painting or sculpture. In music they are more generally gifted than the whites with accurate ears for tune and time, and they have been found capable of imagining a small catch.[15] Whether they will be equal to the composition of a more extensive run of melody, or of complicated harmony, is yet to be proved. Misery is often the parent of the most affecting touches in poetry.—Among the blacks is misery enough, God knows, but no poetry. Love is the peculiar oestrum[16] of the poet. Their love is ardent, but it kindles the senses only, not the imagination. Religion indeed has produced a Phyllis Whately;[17] but it could not produce a poet. The compositions published under her name are below the dignity of criticism. . . .

This unfortunate difference of colour, and perhaps of faculty, is a powerful obstacle to the emancipation of these people. Many of their advocates, while they wish to vindicate the liberty of human nature, are anxious also to preserve its dignity and beauty. Some of these, embarrassed by the question 'What further is to be done with them?' join themselves in opposition with those who are actuated by sordid avarice only. Among the Romans emancipation required but one effort. The slave, when made free, might mix with, without staining the blood of his master. But with us a second is necessary, unknown to history. When freed, he is to be removed beyond the reach of mixture. . . .

There must doubtless be an unhappy influence on the manners of our people produced by the existence of slavery among us. The whole commerce between master and slave is a perpetual exercise of the most boisterous passions, the most unremitting despotism on the

---

[14]*wants*: lacks.

[15]*catch*: simple song. The instrument proper to them is the Banjar, which they brought hither from Africa, and which is the original of the guitar, its chords being precisely the four lower chords of the guitar. [Jefferson's note]

[16]*oestrum*: impulse.

[17]*Phyllis Whately*: Phillis Wheatley.

one part, and degrading submissions on the other. Our children see this, and learn to imitate it; for man is an imitative animal. This quality is the germ[18] of all education in him. From his cradle to his grave he is learning to do what he sees others do. If a parent could find no motive either in his philanthropy[19] or his self-love, for restraining the intemperance of passion towards his slave, it should always be a sufficient one that his child is present. But generally it is not sufficient. The parent storms, the child looks on, catches the lineaments of wrath,[20] puts on the same airs in the circle of smaller slaves, gives a loose to his worst of passions, and thus nursed, educated, and daily exercised in tyranny, cannot but be stamped by it with odious peculiarities. The man must be a prodigy who can retain his manners and morals undepraved by such circumstances. And with what execration[21] should the statesman be loaded, who permitting one half the citizens thus to trample on the rights of the other, transforms those into despots, and these into enemies, destroys the morals of the one part, and the amor patriae[22] of the other. For if a slave can have a country in this world, it must be any other in preference to that in which he is born to live and labour for another: in which he must lock up the faculties of his nature, contribute as far as depends on his individual endeavours to the evanishment[23] of the human race, or entail his own miserable condition on the endless generations proceeding from him. With the morals of the people, their industry also is destroyed. For in a warm climate, no man will labour for himself who can make another labour for him. This is so true, that of the proprietors of slaves a very small proportion indeed are ever seen to labour. And can the liberties of a nation be thought secure when we have removed their only firm basis, a conviction in the minds of the people that these liberties are of the gift of God? That they are not to be violated but with his wrath?

Indeed I tremble for my country when I reflect that God is just: that his justice cannot sleep for ever: that considering numbers, nature and natural means only, a revolution of the wheel of fortune, an exchange of situation, is among possible events: that it may become probable by supernatural interference! The Almighty has no attribute which can take side with us in such a contest.—But it is impossible to be temperate and to pursue this subject through the various considerations

---

[18] *germ*: seed.
[19] *philanthropy*: love of other people.
[20] *lineaments of wrath*: facial features distorted by fury.
[21] *execration*: condemnation.
[22] *amor patriae*: Latin for "love of country."
[23] *evanishment*: extinction.

of policy, of morals, of history natural and civil. We must be contented to hope they will force their way into every one's mind. I think a change already perceptible, since the origin of the present revolution. The spirit of the master is abating,[24] that of the slave rising from the dust, his condition mollifying, the way I hope preparing, under the auspices of heaven, for a total emancipation, and that this is disposed, in the order of events, to be with the consent of the masters, rather than by their extirpation.[25]

[24] *abating*: easing up.
[25] *extirpation*: extermination.

32

BENJAMIN BANNEKER AND THOMAS JEFFERSON

Letters

August 19 and 30, 1791

Benjamin Banneker (1731–1806) was the grandson of a white woman who purchased an African slave named Bannaka, freed him, and married him. Banneker learned the complex art of writing almanacs — annuals that through observation and calculation predicted the following year's lunar cycles, eclipses, and other celestial phenomena. With his knowledge of astronomy, Banneker was hired to assist Andrew Ellicott in surveying the new city of Washington, D.C. About this time he conceived the idea of writing Thomas Jefferson, then secretary of state, enclosing one of his almanacs to disprove Jefferson's public claims about African American intellectual inferiority. On what basis does Banneker make his appeal?

Banneker sent Jefferson his handwritten manuscript of the almanac, rather than a printed copy, to verify that its complex calculations were his own. Jefferson wrote a white friend doubting that Banneker had actually constructed the almanac, but his reply to Banneker was polite.

Copy of a Letter from Benjamin Banneker to the Secretary of State, with His Answer (Philadelphia: Daniel Lawrence, 1792).

Benjamin Banneker to Thomas Jefferson
August 19, 1791

SIR,

I AM fully sensible of the greatness of that freedom, which I take with you on the present occasion; a liberty which seemed to me scarcely allowable, when I reflected on that distinguished and dignified station in which you stand, and the almost general prejudice and prepossession, which is so prevalent in the world against those of my complexion.

I suppose it is a truth too well attested to you, to need a proof here, that we are a race of beings, who have long labored under the abuse and censure of the world; that we have long been looked upon with an eye of contempt; and that we have long been considered rather as brutish than human, and scarcely capable of mental endowments.

Sir, I hope I may safely admit, in consequence of that report which hath reached me, that you are a man far less inflexible in sentiments of this nature, than many others; that you are measurably friendly, and well disposed towards us; and that you are willing and ready to lend your aid and assistance to our relief, from those many distresses, and numerous calamities, to which we are reduced.

Now Sir, if this is founded in truth, I apprehend[1] you will embrace every opportunity, to eradicate that train[2] of absurd and false ideas and opinions, which so generally prevails with respect to us; and that your sentiments are concurrent with mine, which are, that one universal Father hath given being to us all; and that he hath not only made us all of one flesh, but that he hath also, without partiality, afforded us all the same sensations and endowed us all with the same faculties; and that however variable we may be in society or religion, however diversified in situation or color, we are all of the same family, and stand in the same relation to him.

Sir, if these are sentiments of which you are fully persuaded, I hope you cannot but acknowledge, that it is the indispensible duty of those, who maintain for themselves the rights of human nature, and who possess the obligations of Christianity, to extend their power and influence to the relief of every part of the human race, from whatever burden or oppression they may unjustly labor under; and this, I apprehend, a full

[1] *apprehend*: expect.
[2] *train*: long series.

conviction of the truth and obligation of these principles should lead all to.

Sir, I have long been convinced, that if your[3] love for yourselves, and for those inestimable laws, which preserved to you the rights of human nature, was founded on sincerity, you could not but be solicitous, that every individual, of whatever rank or distinction, might with you equally enjoy the blessings thereof; neither could you rest satisfied short of the most active effusion[4] of your exertions, in order to their promotion from any state of degradation, to which the unjustifiable cruelty and barbarism of men may have reduced them. . . .

I ardently hope, that your candor and generosity will plead with you in my behalf, when I make known to you, that it was not originally my design; but having taken up my pen in order to direct to you, as a present, a copy of an Almanac, which I have calculated for the succeeding year, I was unexpectedly and unavoidably led thereto.

This calculation is the production of my arduous study, in this my advanced stage of life; for having long had unbounded desires to become acquainted with the secrets of nature, I have had to gratify my curiosity herein, through my own assiduous application to Astronomical Study, in which I need not recount to you the many difficulties and disadvantages, which I have had to encounter.

And although I had almost declined to make my calculation for the ensuing year, in consequence of that time which I had allotted therefor, being taken up at the Federal Territory,[5] by the request of Mr. Andrew Ellicott, yet finding myself under several engagements to Printers of this state, to whom I had communicated my design, on my return to my place of residence, I industriously applied myself thereto, which I hope I have accomplished with correctness and accuracy; a copy of which I have taken the liberty to direct to you, and which I humbly request you will favorably receive; and although you may have the opportunity of perusing it after its publication, yet I choose to send it to you in manuscript previous thereto, that thereby you might not only have an earlier inspection, but that you might also view it in my own hand writing.

And now, Sir, I shall conclude, and subscribe myself, with the most profound respect,

Your most obedient humble servant,
BENJAMIN BANNEKER.

[3]*your*: white American Revolutionaries'.
[4]*effusion*: outpouring.
[5]*Federal Territory*: Washington, D.C., which Banneker helped survey.

Thomas Jefferson to Benjamin Banneker
August 30, 1791

SIR,

I THANK you, sincerely, for your letter of the 19th instant, and for the Almanac it contained. No body wishes more than I do, to see such proofs as you exhibit, that nature has given to our black brethren talents equal to those of the other colors of men; and that the appearance of the want of them, is owing merely to the degraded condition of their existence, both in Africa and America. I can add with truth, that no body wishes more ardently to see a good system commenced, for raising the condition, both of their body and mind, to what it ought to be, as far as the imbecility[6] of their present existence, and other circumstances, which cannot be neglected, will admit.

I have taken the liberty of sending your Almanac to Monsieur de Condozett,[7] Secretary of the Academy of Sciences at Paris, and Member of the Philanthropic Society, because I considered it as a document, to which your whole color had a right for their justification, against the doubts which have been entertained of them.

I am with great esteem, Sir,

Your most obedient Humble Servant,
THOMAS JEFFERSON.

---

[6]*imbecility*: powerlessness.
[7]*Monsieur de Condozett*: Marquis de Condorcet (1745–1794), a French mathematician and inspector general of the Mint.

33

DAVID GEORGE

An Account of the Life of Mr. David George from Sierra Leone, Africa, Given by Himself

1793

Today more African Americans belong to the Baptist church than to any other denomination. Most historians agree that the nation's first black Baptist church was the one that David George founded at Silver Bluff, South Carolina, in the early 1770s. Born in Essex County, Virginia, in about 1742, George escaped to the British army during the Revolutionary War and emigrated to Nova Scotia in 1783. There he formed that Canadian province's first black Baptist church. Encountering continued persecution in Nova Scotia, more than a thousand black Loyalists, including George, chose to resettle in the British colony of Sierra Leone on the West African coast. He died there in 1810.

I was born in Essex county, Virginia, about 50 or 60 miles from Williamsburg, on Nottaway river, of parents who were brought from Africa, but who had not the fear of God before their eyes. The first work I did was fetching water, and carding of cotton; afterwards I was sent into the field to work about the Indian corn and tobacco, till I was about 19 years old. My father's name was John, and my mother's Judith. I had four brothers, and four sisters, who, with myself, were all born in slavery: our master's name was Chapel—a very bad man to the Negroes.

My older sister was called Patty; I have seen her several times so whipped that her back has been all corruption, as though it would rot. My brother Dick ran away, but they caught him, and brought him home; and as they were going to tie him up, he broke away again, and they hunted him with horses and dogs, till they took him; then they hung him up to a cherry-tree in the yard, by his two hands, quite naked, except his breeches, with his feet about half a yard from the

---

From John Rippon, *The Baptist Annual Register for 1790, 1791, 1792, and Part of 1793...* (London: Dilly, [1793]), 473–84.

ground. They tied his legs close together, and put a pole between them, at one end of which one of the owner's sons sat, to keep him down, and another son at the other. After he had received 500 lashes, or more, they washed his back with salt water, and whipped it in, as well as rubbed it in with a rag; and then directly sent him to work in pulling off the suckers of tobacco. I also have been whipped many a time on my naked skin, and sometimes till the blood has run down over my waistband, but the greatest grief I then had was to see them whip my mother, and to hear her, on her knees, begging for mercy. She was master's cook, and if they only thought she might do any thing better than she did, instead of speaking to her as to a servant, they would strip her directly, and cut away. I believe she was on her death-bed when I got off, but I have never heard since.

Master's rough and cruel usage was the reason of my running-away. Before this time I used to drink, but not steal; did not fear hell, was without knowledge; though I went sometimes to Nottaway, the English church, about eight or nine miles off. I left the plantation about midnight, walked all night, got into Brunswick county, then over Roanoak river, and soon met with some White travelling people, who helped me on to Pedee River. When I had been at work there two or three weeks, a hue and cry[1] found me out, and the master said to me, there are 30 guineas[2] offered for you, but I will have no hand in it: I would advise you to make your way towards Savannah river. I hearkened to him, but was several weeks going.

I worked there, I suppose, as long as two years, with John Green, a white man, before they came after me again. Then I ran away up among the Creek Indians. As I travelled from Savannah river, I came to Okemulgee River, near which the Indians observed my track. They can tell the Black people's track from their own, because they are hollow in the midst of their feet, and the Black's feet are flatter than theirs. They followed my track down to the river, where I was making a [log] raft to cross over with. One of these Indians was a king, called Blue Salt; he could talk a little broken English. He took and carried me away about 17 or 18 miles into the woods to his camp, where they had bear meat, deer meat, turkies, and wild potatoes. I was his prize, and lived with him from the Christmas month till April, when he went into his town Augusta, in the Creek nation. I made fences, dug the ground, planted corn, and worked hard; but the people were kind to me.

---

[1]*hue and cry*: alarm, similar to the modern APB or all points bulletin.
[2]*guineas*: British coins.

S.C. my master's son, came there for me, from Virginia, I suppose 800 miles, and paid King Blue Salt for me in rum, linnen, and a gun; but before he could take me out of the Creek nation, I escaped and went to the Nautchee Indians, and got to live with their King, Jack, who employed me a few weeks. S.C. was waiting this while in hopes to have me. Mr. Gaulfin, who lived on Savannah river, at Silver Bluff, and who was afterwards my master, traded in these parts among the Indians in deer skins. He had a manager here, whose name was John Miller. Mr. Miller knew king Jack, and agreed with him and S.C. as to the price Mr. Gaulfin was to pay for me. So I came away from king Jack, who gave me into the hands of John Miller. Now I mended deer skins, and kept their horses together, that they might not wander too far and be lost. I used also once a year to go down with the horses, carrying deer skins, to Mr. Gaulfins', at Silver Bluff. The distance, I think, was 400 miles, over five or six rivers, which we crossed in leather boats.

After three years, when I came down, I told Mr. Gaulfin, that I wished to live with him at Silver Bluff. He told me I should: so he took me to wait upon him, and was very kind to me. I was with him about four years, I think, before I was married. Here I lived a bad life, and had no serious thoughts about my soul; but after my wife was delivered of our first child, a man of my own color, named Cyrus, who came from Charlestown, South Carolina, to Silver Bluff, told me one day in the woods, That if I lived so, I should never see the face of God in Glory (Whether he himself was a converted man or not, I do not know.) This was the first thing that disturbed me, and gave me much concern. I thought then that I must be saved by prayer. . . .

I got a spelling book and began to read. As Master was a great man, he kept a White school-master to teach the White children to read. I used to go to the little children to teach me a, b, c. They would give me a lesson, which I tried to learn, and then I would go to them again, and ask them if I was right? The reading so ran in my mind, that I think I learned in my sleep as really as when I was awake; and I can now read the Bible, so that what I have in my heart, I can see again in the Scriptures. I continued preaching at Silver Bluff, till the Church, constituted with eight, increased to thirty or more, and till the British came to the city of Savannah and took it. My Master was an Antiloyalist;[3] and being afraid, he now retired from home and left the Slaves behind. My wife and I, and the two children we then had, and fifty or more of my Master's people, went to Ebenezer, about

---

[3] *Antiloyalist*: Patriot.

twenty miles from Savannah, where the King's forces were. The General sent us over the big Ogeechee river to Savages' Plantation, where the White people, who were Loyalists, reported that I was planning to carry the Black people back again to their slavery; and I was thrown into prison, and laid there about a month, when Colonel Brown, belonging to the British, took me out.

I staid some time in Savannah, and at Yamacraw a little distance from it, preaching with brother George Liele. He and I worked together also a month or two: he used to plow, and I to weed Indiancorn. I and my family went into Savannah, at the beginning of the siege. A ball[4] came through the roof of the stable where we lived, and much shattered it, which made us remove to Yamacraw, where we sheltered ourselves under the floor of a house on the ground. Not long after the siege was raised, I caught the small pox, in the fall of the year, and thought I should have died, nor could I do any more than just walk in the spring. My wife used to wash for General Clinton,[5] and out of the little she got maintained us. I was then about a mile from Savannah, when the Americans were coming towards it a second time. I wished my wife to escape, and to take care of herself and of the children, and let me die there. She went: I had about two quarts Indian corn, which I boiled; I ate a little, and a dog came in and devoured the rest; but it pleased God some people who came along the road gave me a little rice: I grew better, and as the troops did not come so near as was expected, I went into Savannah, where I met my family, and tarried there about two years, in a hut belonging to Lawyer Gibbons, where I kept a butcher's stall.

My wife had a brother, who was half an Indian by his mother's side, and half a Negro. He sent us a steer, which I sold, and had now in all 13 dollars, and about three guineas besides, with which I designed to pay our passage, and set off for Charlestown;[6] but the British light horse came in, and took it all away. However as it was a good time for the sale of meat, I borrowed money from some of the Black people to buy hogs, and soon re-paid them, and agreed for a passage to Charlestown, where Major P. the British commander, was very kind to me. When the English were going to evacuate Charlestown, they advised me to go to Halifax, in Nova Scotia,[7] and gave the few Black people, and it may be as many as 500 White people, their passage for nothing.

---

[4] *ball*: cannon ball.
[5] *General Clinton*: British commander Henry Clinton.
[6] *Charlestown*: Charleston, South Carolina.
[7] *Nova Scotia*: peninsular province on the Atlantic coast of Canada.

We were 22 days on the passage, and used very ill[8] on board. When we came off Halifax, I got leave to go ashore. On shewing my papers to General Patterson, he sent orders, by a Serjeant, for my wife and children to follow me. This was before Christmas, and we staid there till June; but as no way was open for me to preach to my own color, I got leave to go to Shelburne (150 miles, or more, I suppose, by sea) in the suit of General Patterson, leaving my wife and children for a while behind.

Numbers of my color were here, but I found the White people were against me. I began to sing the first night, in the woods, at a camp, for there were no houses then built; they were just clearing and preparing to erect a town. The Black people came far and near, it was so new to them; I kept on so every night in the week, and appointed a meeting for the first Lord's-day, in a valley between two hills, close by the river; and a great number of White and Black people came, and I was so overjoyed with having an opportunity once more of preaching the word of God, that after I had given out the hymn, I could not speak for tears. In the afternoon we met again, in the same place, and I had great liberty from the Lord. We had a meeting now every evening, and those poor creatures who had never heard the gospel before, listened to me very attentively: but the White people, the justices, and all, were in an uproar, and said that I might go out into the woods, for I should not stay there. I ought to except one White man, who knew me at Savannah, and who said I should have his lot to live upon as long as I would, and build a house if I pleased. I then cut down poles, stripped bark, and made a smart hut, and the people came flocking to the preaching every evening for a month, as though they had come for their supper. . . . At this time a White person, William Holmes, who, with Deborah his wife, had been converted by reading the scriptures, and lived at Jones's Harbour, about twenty miles down the river, came up for me, and would have me go away with him in his schooner to his house. I went with him, first to his own house, and then to a town they called Liverpool, inhabited by White people. Many had been baptized there by Mr. Chippenham, of Annapolis, in Nova Scotia. Mr. Jesse Dexter preached to them, but was not their pastor. It is a mixed communion church. I preached there; the Christians were all alive, and we had a little heaven together. We then returned to brother Holmes's, and he and his wife came up with me to Shelburn, and gave their experiences to the church on Thursday, and were baptized on Lord's-day. Their relations who lived in the town were very angry, raised a mob, and endeavoured to hinder their being baptized. Mrs. Holmes's sister especially laid hold of her hair to keep her

---

[8]*used very ill*: treated very badly.

from going down into the water; but the justices commanded peace, and said that she should be baptized, as she herself desired it. Then they were all quiet. Soon after this the persecution increased, and became so great, that it did not seem possible to preach, and I thought I must leave Shelburn. Several of the black people had houses upon my lot, but forty or fifty disbanded soldiers were employed, who came with the tackle of ships, and turned my dwelling house, and every one of their houses, quite over; and the Meeting house they would have burned down, had not the ring-leader of the mob himself prevented it.

But I continued to preaching in it till they came one night, and stood before the pulpit, and swore how they would treat me if I preached again. But I stayed and preached, and the next day they came and beat me with sticks, and drove me into a swamp. I returned in the evening, and took my wife and children over to the river to Birch town, where some Black people were settled, and there seemed a greater prospect of doing good than at Shelburn, I preached at Birchtown from the fall till about the middle of December, and was frequently hearing experiences, and baptized about twenty there. Those who desired to hear the word of God, invited me from house to house, and so I preached. A little before Christmas, as my own color persecuted me there, I set off with my family, to return to Shelburn; and coming down the river the boat was frozen, but we took whip-saws and cut away the ice till we came to Shelburne. In my absence the Meeting house was occupied by a sort of a tavern-keeper, who said, "The old Negro wanted to make a heaven of this place, but I'll make a hell of it. Then I preached in it as before, and as my house was pulled down, lived in it also. The people began to attend again, and in the summer there was a considerable revival of religion. Now I went down about twenty miles to a place called Ragged Island, among some White people, who desired to hear the word. One White sister was converted there while I was preaching concerning the disciples, who left all and followed Christ. She came up afterwards, gave her experience to our church, and was baptized, and two Black sisters with her. Then her other sister gave in her experience, and joined us without Baptism, to which she would have submitted, had not her family cruelly hindered her. . . .

The next fall, Agent (afterwards Governor) Clarkson came to Halifax, about settling the new colony at Sierra Leone. The White people in Nova Scotia were very unwilling that we should go, though they had been very cruel to us, and treated many of us as bad as though we had been slaves. They attempted to persuade us that if we went away we should be slaves again. The brethren and sisters all round at St. John's, Halifax, and other places, Mr. Wesley's people and all, consulted what was best to do, and sent in their names to me, to give to Mr. Clarkson, and I was to tell him that they were willing to go. I carried him their names, and he appointed to meet us at Birch Town the next day. We gathered together there, in the Meeting-house of brother Moses, a blind man, one of Mr. Wesley's preachers. Then the Governor read the proclamation, which contained what was offered, in case we had a mind willingly to go, and the greatest part of us were pleased and agreed to go. We appointed a day over at Shelburn, when the names were to be given to the Governor. Almost all the Baptists went, except a few of the sisters whose husbands were inclined to go back to New York, and sister Lizze, a Quebec Indian, and brother Lewis, her husband, who was an half Indian, both of whom were converted under my ministry, and had been baptized by me. There are a few scattered Baptists yet at Shelburn, St. John's, Jones's Harbour, and Ragged Island, beside the congregations at the other places I mentioned before. The meeting-house lot, and all our land at Shelburn, it may be half an acre, was sold to merchant Black for about £7.

We departed and called at Liverpool, a place I mentioned before. I preached a farewel sermon there; I longed to do it. Before I left the town, Major Collins, who with his wife were to hear me at this place; was very kind to me, and gave me some salted herrings, which were very acceptable all the way to Sierra Leone. We sailed from Liverpool to Halifax, where we tarried three or four weeks, and I preached from house to house, and my farewel sermon in Mr. Marchington's Methodist Meeting-house. There is also a Mr. William Black, at Halifax, a smart preacher, one of Mr. Wesley's, who baptizes those Christians who desire it by immersion.

Our passage from Halifax to Sierra Leone was seven weeks, in which we had very stormy weather. Several persons died on the voyage, of a catching fever, among whom were three of my Elders, Sampson Colwell, a loving man, Peter Richards, and John Williams.

There was great joy to see the land. The high mountain, at some distance from Free-town, where we now live, appeared like a cloud to us. I preached the first Lord's day, it was a blessed time, under a sail, and so I did for several weeks after. We then erected a hovel for a Meeting-house, which is made of posts put into the ground, and poles over our heads, which are covered with grass. While I was preaching under the sails, sisters Patty Webb and Lucy Lawrence were converted, and they, with old sister Peggy, brother Bill Taylor, and brother Sampson Haywood, three who were awakened before they came this voyage, have since been baptized in the river.

On the voyage from Halifax to Sierra Leone, I asked the Governor if I might not hereafter go to England? and some time after we arrived there, I told him I wished to see the Baptist brethren who live in his country. He was a very kind man to me and to every body; he is very free and good natured, and used to come to hear me preach, and would sometimes sit down at our private meetings; and he liked that I should call my last child by his name. And I sent to Mr. Henry Thornton, O what a blessed man is that! he is brother, father, every thing. He ordered me five guineas, and I had leave to come over. When I came away from Sierra Leone, I preached a farewel sermon to the church, and encouraged them to look to the Lord, and submit to one another, and regard what is said to them by my three Elders, brethren Hector Peters, and John Colbert, who are two exhorters; and brother John Ramsey.

34

BOSTON KING

Memoirs of the Life of Boston King,
A Black Preacher, Written by Himself

July 4, 1796

Among the African American slaves who gained freedom by fighting for the British was Boston King, born near Charleston, South Carolina, in about 1760. After the war, he joined the African American exodus to Nova Scotia, where he experienced a religious conversion and became a Methodist minister. In 1792 he accompanied some 1,200 other black Loyalists who resettled in Sierra Leone. He spent much of the mid-1790s preaching and studying in England. Here King recounts his adventures as a soldier and his life in Sierra Leone, where he would die in 1802.

It is by no means an agreeable task to write an account of my Life, yet my gratitude to Almighty GOD, who considered my affliction, and

"Memoirs of the Life of Boston King, A Black Preacher, Written by Himself...,"
Methodist Magazine, for the Year 1798 21 (1798): 105–10, 157, 263–65.

looked upon me in my low estate, who delivered me from the hand of the oppressor, and established my goings, impels me to acknowledge his goodness: And the importunity of many respectable friends, whom I highly esteem, have induced me to set down, as they occurred to my memory, a few of the most striking incidents I have met with in my pilgrimage. I am well aware of my inability for such an undertaking, having only a slight acquaintance with the language in which I write, and being obliged to snatch a few hours, now and then, from pursuits, which to me, perhaps, are more profitable. However, such as it is, I present it to the Friends of Religion and Humanity, hoping that it will be of some use to mankind.

I was born in the Province of South Carolina, 28 miles from Charles-Town. My father was stolen away from Africa when he was young. I have reason to believe that he lived in the fear and love of GOD. He attended to that true Light which lighteth every man that cometh into the world. He lost no opportunity of hearing the Gospel, and never omitted praying with his family every night. He likewise read to them, and to as many as were inclined to hear. On the Lord's-Day he rose very early, and met his family: After which he worked in the field till about three in the afternoon, and then went into the woods and read till sun-set: The slaves being obliged to work on the Lord's-Day to procure such things as were not allowed by their masters. He was beloved by his master, and had the charge of the Plantation as a driver for many years. In his old age he was employed as a mill-cutter. Those who knew him, say, that they never heard him swear an oath, but on the contrary, he reproved all who spoke improper words in his hearing. To the utmost of his power he endeavoured to make his family happy, and his death was a very great loss to us all. My mother was employed chiefly in attending upon those that were sick, having some knowledge of the virtue of herbs, which she learned from the Indians. She likewise had the care of making the people's clothes, and on these accounts was indulged with many privileges which the rest of the slaves were not.

When I was six years old I waited in the house upon my master. In my 9th year I was put to mind the cattle. Here I learnt from my comrades the horrible sin of Swearing and Cursing. When 12 years old, it pleased GOD to alarm me by a remarkable dream. At mid-day, when the cattle went under the shade of the trees, I dreamt that the world was on fire, and that I saw the supreme Judge descend on his great white Throne! I saw millions of millions of souls; some of whom ascended up to heaven; while others were rejected, and fell into the greatest confusion and despair. This dream made such an impression upon my mind, that I refrained from swearing and bad company, and from that time acknowledged that there was a GOD; but how to serve GOD I knew not. Being obliged to travel in different parts of America with race-horses, I suffered many hardships. Happening one time to lose a boot belonging to the Groom, he would not suffer me to have any shoes all that Winter, which was a great punishment to me.

When 16 years old, I was bound apprentice to a trade. . . .

My master being apprehensive that Charles-Town was in danger on account of the war, removed into the country, about 38 miles off. Here we built a large house for Mr. Waters, during which time the English took Charles-Town. Having obtained leave one day to see my parents, who lived about 12 miles off, and it being late before I could go, I was obliged to borrow one of Mr. Waters's horses; but a servant of my master's, took the horse from me to go a little journey, and stayed two or three days longer than he ought. This involved me in the greatest perplexity, and I expected the severest punishment, because the gentleman to whom the horse belonged was a very bad man, and knew not how to shew mercy.

To escape his cruelty, I determined to go to Charles-Town, and throw myself into the hands of the English. They received me readily, and I began to feel the happiness of liberty, of which I knew nothing before, altho' I was much grieved at first, to be obliged to leave my friends, and reside among strangers. In this situation I was seized with the smallpox, and suffered great hardships; for all the Blacks affected with that disease, were ordered to be carried a mile from the camp, lest the soldiers should be infected, and disabled from marching. This was a grievous circumstance to me and many others. We lay sometimes a whole day without any thing to eat or drink; but Providence sent a man, who belonged to the York volunteers whom I was acquainted with, to my relief. He brought me such things as I stood in need of; and by the blessing of the Lord I began to recover.

By this time, the English left the place; but as I was unable to march with the army, I expected to be taken by the enemy. However when they came, and understood that we were ill of the small-pox, they precipitately left us for fear of the infection. Two days after, the waggons were sent to convey us to the English Army, and we were put into a little cottage, (being 25 in number) about a quarter of a mile from the Hospital.

Being recovered, I marched with the army to Chamblem. When we came to the head-quarters, our regiment was 35 miles off. I stayed at the head-quarters three weeks, during which time our regiment had an engagement with the Americans, and the man who relieved me when I was ill of the small-pox, was wounded in the battle, and brought to the hospital. As soon as I heard of his misfortune, I went to see him, and tarried with him in the hospital six weeks, till he recovered; rejoicing that it was in my power to return him the kindness he had shewed me. . . .

Our situation was very precarious, and we expected to be made prisoners every day; for the Americans had 1600 men, not far off; whereas our whole number amounted only to 250: But there were 1200 English about 30 miles off; only we knew not how to inform them of our danger, as the Americans were in possession of the country. Our commander at length determined to send me with a letter, promising me great rewards, if I was successful in the business, I refused going on horse-back, and set off on foot about 3 o'clock in the afternoon; I expected every moment to fall in with the enemy, whom I well knew would shew me no mercy. I went on without interruption, till I got within six miles of my journey's end, and then was alarmed with a great noise a little before me. But I stepped out of the road, and fell flat upon my face till they were gone by. I then arose, and praised the Name of the Lord for his great mercy, and again pursued my journey, till I came to Mums-corner tavern. I knocked at the door, but they blew out the candle. I knocked again, and intreated the master to open the door. At last he came with a frightful countenance, and said, "I thought it was the Americans; for they were here about an hour ago, and I thought they were returned again." I asked, How many were there? he answered, "about one hundred." I desired him to saddle his horse for me, which he did, and went with me himself. When we had gone about two miles, we were stopped by the picket-guard, till the Captain came out with 30 men: As soon as he knew that I had brought an express from Nelson's-Ferry, he received me with great kindness, and expressed his approbation of my courage and conduct in this dangerous business. Next morning, Colonel Small gave me three shillings, and many fine promises, which were all that I ever received for this service from him. However he sent 600 men to relieve the troops at Nelson's-ferry.

Soon after I went to Charles-Town, and entered on board a man of war. As we were going to Chesepeak-bay, we were at the taking of a rich prize.[1] We stayed in the bay two days, and then sailed for New-York, where I went on shore. Here I endeavoured to follow my trade, but for want of tools was obliged to relinquish it, and enter into service. But the wages were so low that I was not able to keep myself in

---

[1] *taking of a rich prize*: capture of a valuable enemy ship.

clothes, so that I was under the necessity of leaving my master and going to another. I stayed with him four months, but he never paid me, and I was obliged to leave him also, and work about the town until I was married. A year after I was taken very ill, but the Lord raised me up again in about five weeks. I then went out in a pilot-boat.[2] We were at sea eight days, and had only provisions for five, so that we were in danger of starving. On the 9th day we were taken by an American whale-boat. I went on board them with a chearful countenance, and asked for bread and water, and made very free with them. They carried me to Brunswick,[3] and used me well. Notwithstanding which, my mind was sorely distressed at the thought of being again reduced to slavery, and separated from my wife and family; and at the same time it was exceeding difficult to escape from my bondage, because the river at Amboy[4] was above a mile over, and likewise another to cross at Staten-Island. I called to remembrance the many great deliverances the Lord had wrought for me, and besought him to save me this once, and I would serve him all the days of my life.

While my mind was thus exercised, I went into the jail to see a lad whom I was acquainted with at New-York. He had been taken prisoner, and attempted to make his escape, but was caught 12 miles off: They tied him to the tail of a horse, and in this manner brought him back to Brunswick. When I saw him, his feet were fastened in the stocks, and at night both his hands. This was a terrifying sight to me, as I expected to meet with the same kind of treatment, if taken in the act of attempting to regain my liberty. I was thankful that I was not confined in a jail, and my master used me as well as I could expect; and indeed the slaves about Baltimore, Philadelphia, and New-York, have as good victuals as many of the English; for they have meat once a day, and milk for breakfast and supper; and what is better than all, many of the masters send their slaves to school at night, that they may learn to read the Scriptures. This is a privilege indeed. But alas, all these enjoyments could not satisfy me without liberty! Sometimes I thought, if it was the will of GOD that I should be a slave, I was ready to resign myself to his will; but at other times I could not find the least desire to content myself in slavery.

Being permitted to walk about when my work was done, I used to go to the ferry, and observed, that when it was low water the people waded across the river; tho' at the same time I saw there were guards

---

[2] *pilot-boat*: a small boat that guides larger ships into harbor.
[3] *Brunswick*: New Brunswick, New Jersey.
[4] *Amboy*: Perth Amboy, New Jersey.

posted at the place to prevent the escape of prisoners and slaves. As I was at prayer one Sunday evening, I thought the Lord heard me, and would mercifully deliver me. Therefore putting my confidence in him, about one o'clock in the morning I went down to the river side, and found the guards were either asleep or in the tavern. I instantly entered into the river, but when I was a little distance from the opposite shore, I heard the sentinels disputing among themselves: One said, "I am sure I saw a man cross the river." Another replied, "There is no such thing." It seems they were afraid to fire at me, or make an alarm, lest they should be punished for their negligence. When I had got a little distance from the shore, I fell down upon my knees, and thanked GOD for this deliverance. I travelled till about five in the morning, and then concealed myself till seven o'clock at night, when I proceeded forward, thro' bushes and marshes, near the road, for fear of being discovered. When I came to the river, opposite Staten-Island, I found a boat; and altho' it was very near a whale-boat, yet I ventured into it, and cutting the rope, got safe over. The commanding officer, when informed of my case, gave me a passport, and I proceeded to New-York.

When I arrived at New-York, my friends rejoiced to see me once more restored to liberty, and joined me in praising the Lord for his mercy and goodness. But notwithstanding this great deliverance, and the promises I had made to serve GOD, yet my good resolutions soon vanished away like the morning dew: The love of this world extinguished my good desires, and stole away my heart from GOD, so that I rested in a mere form of religion for near three years. About which time, (in 1783,) the horrors and devastation of war happily terminated, and peace was restored between America and Great Britain, which diffused universal joy among all parties, except us, who had escaped from slavery, and taken refuge in the English army; for a report prevailed at New-York, that all the slaves, in number 2000, were to be delivered up to their masters, altho' some of them had been three or four years among the English. This dreadful rumour filled us all with inexpressible anguish and terror, especially when we saw our old masters coming from Virginia, North-Carolina, and other parts, and seizing upon their slaves in the streets of New-York, or even dragging them out of their beds. Many of the slaves had very cruel masters, so that the thoughts of returning home with them embittered life to us. For some days we lost our appetite for food, and sleep departed from our eyes. The English had compassion upon us in the day of distress, and issued out a Proclamation, importing, That all slaves should be free, who had taken refuge in the British lines, and claimed the sanction and privileges of the Proclamations respecting the security and protection of Negroes. In consequence of this, each of us received a certificate from the commanding officer at New-York, which dispelled all our fears, and filled us with joy and gratitude. Soon after, ships were fitted out, and furnished with every necessary for conveying us to Nova Scotia. We arrived at Burch Town in the month of August, where we all safely landed. Every family had a lot of land, and we exerted all our strength in order to build comfortable huts before the cold weather set in. . . .

[King accepted the British government's offer to resettle in Sierra Leone on the West African coast.]

The people regularly attended the means of Grace, and the work of the Lord prospered. When the rains were over, we erected a small chapel, and went on our way comfortably. I worked for the Company, for 3s.[5] per day, and preached in my turn. I likewise found my mind drawn out to pity the native inhabitants, and preached to them several times, but laboured under great inconveniencies to make them understand the Word of GOD, as I could only visit them on the Lord's-Day. I therefore went to the Governor, and solicited him to give me employment in the Company's Plantation on Bullam Shore, in order that I might have frequent opportunities of conversing with the Africans. He kindly approved of my intention, and sent me to the Plantation to get ship-timber in company with several others.

The gentleman who superintended the Plantation, treated me with the utmost kindness, and allowed six men to help me to build a house for myself, which we finished in 12 days. When a sufficient quantity of timber was procured, and other business for the Company in this place compleated, I was sent to the African town to teach the children to read, but found it difficult to procure scholars, as the parents shewed no great inclination to send their children. I therefore said to them, on the Lord's-Day after preaching, "It is a good thing that GOD has made the White People, and that he has inclined their hearts to bring us into this country, to teach you his ways, and to tell you that he gave his Son to die for you; and if you will obey his commandments he will make you happy in this world, and in that which is to come; where you will live with him in heaven;—and all pain and wretchedness will be at an end;—and you shall enjoy peace without interruption,

---

[5]*s.*: shillings, British currency unit.

joy without bitterness, and happiness to all eternity. The Almighty not only invites you to come unto him, but also points out the way whereby you may find his favour, viz. turn from your wicked ways, cease to do evil, and learn to do well. He now affords you a means which you never had before; he gives you his Word to be a light to your feet, and a lantern to your paths; and he likewise gives you an opportunity of having your children instructed in the Christian Religion. But if you neglect to send them, you must be answerable to GOD for it."

The poor Africans appeared attentive to the exhortation, altho' I laboured under the disadvantage of using an interpreter. My scholars soon increased from four to twenty; fifteen of whom continued with me five months. I taught them the Alphabet, and to spell words of two syllables; and likewise the Lord's-Prayer. And I found them as apt to learn as any children I have known. But with regard to the old people, I am doubtful whether they will ever abandon the evil habits in which they were educated, unless the Lord visits them in some extraordinary manner.

In the year 1793, the gentlemen belonging to the Company told me, that if I would consent to go to England with the Governor, he would procure me two or three years schooling, that I might be better qualified to teach the natives. When this proposal was first mentioned to me, it seemed like an idle tale; but upon further conversation on the subject, difficulties were removed, and I consented. On the 26th of March 1794, we embarked for England, and arrived at Plymouth, after a pleasant voyage, on the 16th of May. On the 1st of June we got into the Thames, and soon after, Mrs. Paul, whom I was acquainted with in America, came to Wapping, and invited me to the New Chapel in the City-Road, where I was kindly received.

When I first arrived in England, I considered my great ignorance and inability, and that I was among a wise and judicious people, who were greatly my superiors in knowledge and understanding; these reflections had such an effect upon me, that I formed a resolution never to attempt to preach while I stayed in the country; but the kind importunity of the Preachers and others removed my objections, and I found it profitable to my own soul, to be exercised in inviting sinners to Christ; particularly one Sunday, while I was preaching at Snowsfields-Chapel, the Lord blessed me abundantly, and I found a more cordial love to the White People than I had ever experienced before. In the former part of my life I had suffered greatly from the cruelty and injustice of the Whites, which induced me to look upon them, in general, as our enemies: And even after the Lord had manifested his forgiving mercy to me, I still felt at times an uneasy distrust and shyness towards them;

but on that day the Lord removed all my prejudices; for which I bless his holy Name.

In the month of August 1794, I went to Bristol; and from thence Dr. Coke took me with him to Kingswood-School, where I continued to the present time, and have endeavoured to acquire all the knowledge I possibly could, in order to be useful in that sphere which the blessed hand of Providence may conduct me into, if my life is spared. I have great cause to be thankful that I came to England, for I am now fully convinced, that many of the White People, instead of being enemies and oppressors of us poor Blacks, are our friends, and deliverers from slavery, as far as their ability and circumstances will admit. I have met with the most affectionate treatment from the Methodists of London, Bristol, and other places which I have had an opportunity of visiting. And I must confess, that I did not believe there were upon the face of the earth a people so friendly and humane as I have proved them to be. I beg leave to acknowledge the obligations I am under to Dr. Coke, Mr. Bradford, and all the Preachers and people; and I pray GOD to reward them a thousand fold for all the favours they have shewn to me in a strange land.

BOSTON KING
Kingswood-School, June 4, 1796.

35

JACOB NICHOLSON AND OTHER FORMER SLAVES FROM NORTH CAROLINA

Petition to Congress
January 23, 1797

The authors of this petition, all former slaves from North Carolina, asked Congress for a redress of their grievances. North Carolina, like several other southern states, forced manumitted slaves to leave the state. This requirement frequently broke up their families and caused other hardships, as the petitioners, one by one, describe in detail.

From *Annals of Congress*, House of Representatives, 4th Congress, 2nd Session, 2015–17.

To the President, Senate, and House of Representatives.

The Petition and Representation of the under-named Freemen, respectfully showeth: —

That, being of African descent, late inhabitants and natives of North Carolina, to you only, under God, can we apply with any hope of effect, for redress of our grievances, having been compelled to leave the State wherein we had a right of residence, as freemen liberated under the hand and seal of humane and conscientious masters, the validity of which act of justice, in restoring us to our native right of freedom, was confirmed by judgment of the Superior Court of North Carolina, wherein it was brought to trial; yet, not long after this decision, a law of that State was enacted, under which men of cruel disposition, and void of just principle, received countenance and authority in violently seizing, imprisoning, and selling into slavery, such as had been so emancipated; whereby we were reduced to the necessity of separating from some of our nearest and most tender connexions, and of seeking refuge in such parts of the Union where more regard is paid to the public declaration in favor of liberty and the common right of men, several hundreds, under our circumstances, having, in consequence of the said law, been hunted day and night, like beasts of the forest, by armed men with dogs, and made a prey of as free and lawful plunder. Among others thus exposed, I, Jupiter Nicholson, of Perquimans county, North Carolina, after being set free by my master, Thomas Nicholson, and having been about two years employed as a seaman in the service of Zachary Nickson, on coming on shore, was pursued by men with dog and arms; but was favored to escape by night to Virginia, with my wife, who was manumitted by Gabriel Cosand, where I resided about four years in the town of Portsmouth, chiefly employed in sawing boards and scantling; from thence I removed with my wife to Philadelphia, where I have been employed, at times, by water, working along shore, or sawing wood. I left behind me a father and mother, who were manumitted by Thomas Nicholson and Zachary Dickson; they have been since taken up, with a beloved brother, and sold into cruel bondage.

I, Jacob Nicholson, also of North Carolina, being set free by my master, Joseph Nicholson, but continuing to live with him till, being pursued day and night, I was obliged to leave my abode, sleep in the woods, and stacks[1] in the fields, &c., to escape the hands of violent

---

[1] *stacks*: haystacks.

men who, induced by the profit afforded them by law, followed this course as a business; at length, by night, I made my escape, leaving a mother, one child, and two brothers, to see whom I dare not return.

I, Job Albert, manumitted by Benjamin Albertson, who was my careful guardian to protect me from being afterwards taken and sold, providing me with a house to accommodate me and my wife, who was liberated by William Robertson; but we were night and day hunted by men armed with guns, swords, and pistols, accompanied with mastiff dogs; from whose violence, being one night apprehensive of immediate danger, I left my dwelling, locked and barred, and fastened with a chain, being at some distance from it, while my wife was by my kind master locked up under his roof. I heard them break into my house, where, not finding their prey, they got but a small booty, a handkerchief of about a dollar value, and some provisions; but, not long after, I was discovered and seized by Alexander Stafford, William Stafford, and Thomas Creesy, who were armed with guns and clubs. After binding me with my hands behind me, and a rope round my arms and body, they took me about four miles to Hartford prison, where I lay four weeks, suffering much for want of provision; from thence, with the assistance of a fellow-prisoner, (a white man,) I made my escape, and for three dollars was conveyed, with my wife, by a humane person, in a covered wagon by night, to Virginia, where, in the neighborhood of Portsmouth, I continued unmolested about four years, being chiefly engaged in sawing boards and plank. On being advised to move Northward, I came with my wife to Philadelphia, where I have labored for a livelihood upwards of two years, in Summer mostly, along shore in vessels and stores, and sawing wood in the Winter. My mother was set free by Phineas Nickson, my sister by John Trueblood, and both taken up and sold into slavery, myself deprived of the consolation of seeing them, without being exposed to the like grievous oppression.

I, Thomas Pritchet, was set free by my master Thomas Pritchet, who furnished me with land to raise provisions for my use, where I built myself a house, cleared a sufficient spot of woodland to produce ten bushels of corn; the second year about fifteen, and the third, had as much planted as I suppose would have produced thirty bushels; this I was obliged to leave about one month before it was fit for gathering, being threatened by Holland Lockwood, who married my said master's widow, that if I would not come and serve him, he would apprehend me, and send me to the West Indies; Enoch Ralph also threatening to send me to jail, and sell me for the good of the country:[2] being thus in jeopardy, I left my little farm, with my small stock and utensils, and my corn standing, and escaped by night into Virginia, where shipping myself for Boston, I was, through stress of weather landed in New York, where I served as a waiter for seventeen months; but my mind being distressed on account of the situation of my wife and children, I returned to Norfolk in Virginia, with a hope of at least seeing them, if I could not obtain their freedom; but finding I was advertised in the newspaper, twenty dollars the reward for apprehending me, my dangerous situation obliged me to leave Virginia, disappointed of seeing my wife and children, coming to Philadelphia, where I resided in the employment of a waiter upward of two years.

In addition to the hardship of our own case, as above set forth, we believe ourselves warranted, on the present occasion, in offering to your consideration the singular case of a fellow-black now confined in the jail of this city, under sanction of the act of General Government, called the Fugitive Law, as it appears to us a flagrant proof how far human beings, merely on account of color and complexion, are, through prevailing prejudice, outlawed and excluded from common justice and common humanity, by the operation of such partial laws in support of habits and customs cruelly oppressive. This man, having been many years past manumitted by his master in North Carolina, was under the authority of the aforementioned law of that State, sold again into slavery, and, after having served his purchaser upwards of six years, made his escape to Philadelphia, where he has resided eleven years, having a wife and our children; and, by an agent of the Carolina claimer, has been lately apprehended and committed to prison, his said claimer, soon after the man's escaping from him, having advertised him, offering a reward of ten silver dollars to any person that would bring him back, or five times that sum to any person that would make due proof of his being killed, and no questions asked by whom.

---

[2]*for the good of the country*: with the profits going to the state government.

36

PROSSER'S BEN AND OTHER SLAVES

Testimony against Gabriel

October 6, 1800

In 1800, Gabriel, a blacksmith owned by Thomas Prosser of Henrico County, just outside Richmond, Virginia's state capital, set in motion one of the most wide-ranging slave insurrection conspiracies in American history. More than six hundred slaves were alleged to have been involved. Some of the participants revealed the plot to white authorities—one of the few ways slaves could obtain freedom was by exposing such conspiracies— and the rebellion was suppressed before it began. One prisoner hanged himself in his cell. Twenty-six were executed, the last being Gabriel himself. Judges took testimony—some of it questionable, given the circumstances under which it was extracted—from many of the slave rebels.

Prosser's Ben—Gabriel was appointed Captain at first consultation respecting the Insurrection, and afterwards when he had enlisted a number of men was appointed General. That they were to kill Mr. Prosser, Mr. Mosby, and all the neighbors, and then proceed to Richmond, where they would kill everybody, take the treasury, and divide the money amongst the soldiers; after which he would fortify Richmond and proceed to discipline[1] his men, as he apprehended force would be raised elsewhere to repel him. That if the white people agreed to their freedom they would then hoist a white flag, and he would dine and drink with the merchants of the city on the day when it should be agreed to.

Gabriel enlisted a number of negroes. The prisoner[2] went with the witness[3] to Mr. Young's to see Ben Woolfolk, who was going to Caroline to enlist men there. He gave three shillings for himself and three other negroes, to be expended in recruiting men.

[1] *discipline*: command.
[2] *the prisoner*: the person being tried for participating in the rebellion (in this case, Gabriel).
[3] *the witness*: the person whose testimony is recorded here.

H. W. Flournoy, ed., *Calendar of Virginia State Papers...*, Vol. IX (Richmond, Va.: James E. Goode, 1890), 164–65.

The prisoner made the handles of the swords, which were made by Solomon. The prisoner shewed the witness a quantity of bullets, nearly a peck,[4] which he and Martin had run, and some lead then on hand, and he said he had ten pounds of powder[5] which he had purchased. Gabriel said he had nearly 10,000 men; he had 1,000 in Richmond, about 600 in Caroline, and nearly 500 at the Coal pits, besides others at different places, and that he expected the poor white people would also join him, and that two Frenchmen had actually joined, whom he said Jack Ditcher knew, but whose names he would not mention to the witness. That the prisoner had enlisted nearly all the negroes in town as he said, and amongst them had 400 Horsemen. That in consequence of the bad weather on Saturday night, an agreement was made to meet at the Tobacco House of Mr. Prosser the ensuing night. Gabriel said all the negroes from Petersburg were to join him after he had commenced the Insurrection.

Mr. Price's John—He saw the prisoner at a meeting, who gave a general invitation to the negro men to attend at the Spring to drink grog.[6] That when there he mentioned the Insurrection, and proposed that all present should join them in the same, and meet in 3 weeks for the purpose of carrying the same into effect, and enjoined[7] several of the negroes then present to use the best of their endeavors in enlisting men, and to meet according to the time appointed.

Ben. Woolfolk—The prisoner was present at the meeting at Mr. Young's, who came to get persons to join him to carry on the war against the white people. That after meeting they adjourned to the Spring and held a consultation, when it was concluded that in 3 weeks the business should commence. Gabriel said he had 12 dozen swords made, and had worn out 2 pair of bullet moulds in running bullets, and pulling a third pair out of his pocket, observed that was nearly worn out. That Bob Cooley and Mr. Tinsley's Jim was to let them into the Capitol to get the arms out. That the lower part of the Town towards Rocketts was to be fired,[8] which would draw forth the citizens (that part of the town being of little value); this would give an opportunity to the negroes to seize on the arms and ammunition, and then they would commence the attack upon them. After the assembling of the negroes near Prosser's, and previous to their coming to Richmond, a company was to be sent to Gregorie's Tavern to take possession of

[4] *peck*: eight quarts or one-fourth of a bushel.
[5] *powder*: gunpowder.
[6] *grog*: a cheap alcoholic drink.
[7] *enjoined*: called upon.
[8] *fired*: set ablaze.

some arms there deposited. The prisoner said, at the time of meeting the witness at Mr. Young's, that he had the evening before received six Guns—one of which he had delivered to Col. Wilkinson's Sam. That he was present when Gabriel was appointed General and Geo. Smith second in command. That none were to be spared of the whites except Quakers, Methodists, and French people. The prisoner and Gilbert concluded to purchase a piece of silk for a flag, on which they would have written "death or Liberty."...

37

PAUL CUFFEE

Memoir of Captain Paul Cuffee
October 1811

The son of a Wampanoag Indian woman and an Africa-born slave who managed to purchase his freedom, Paul Cuffee (1759–1817) was born free on an island that was part of Massachusetts. In Akan, a West African language, the name "Cuffee" means "Friday." Paul Cuffee went to sea as a sailor at age sixteen and eventually was able to purchase and captain ships of his own—and even to hire other men, black and white, as captains. Cuffee despaired of ever living on good terms with whites in Massachusetts, however, and he dreamed of resettling in Africa with some of his fellow free blacks. He made several trips to the British colony of Sierra Leone and finally settled thirty-eight African Americans there. He might have emigrated himself, but his wife was opposed to the idea. In 1780 Cuffee and others petitioned the Massachusetts legislature against taxation without representation (Document 21). Note the reference to that petition in this memoir.

"On the first of the present month of August, 1811, a vessel arrived at Liverpool, with a cargo from Sierra Leone, the owner, master, mate, and whole crew of which are free Negroes. The master, who is also owner, is the son of an American Slave, and is said to be very well skilled both in trade and navigation, as well as to be of a very pious and moral character. It must have been a strange and animating[1] spectacle to see this free and enlightened African entering, as an independent trader, with his black crew, into that port which was so lately the *nidus*[2] of the Slave Trade."—*Edinb[urgh] Review, August*, 1811.

We are happy in having an opportunity of confirming the above account, and at the same time of laying before our readers an authentic memoir of Capt. Paul Cuffee, the master and owner of the vessel above referred to, who sailed from this port on the 20th ult.[3] *with a licence from the British Government, to prosecute his intended voyage to Sierra Leone.*

THE father of Paul Cuffee, was a native of Africa, whence he was brought as a Slave into Massachusetts. He was there purchased by a person named Slocum, and remained in slavery a considerable portion of his life. He was named Cuffee, but as it is usual in those parts took the name of Slocum, as expressing to whom he belonged. Like many of his countrymen he possessed a mind superior to his condition, and although he was diligent in the business of his Master and faithful to his interest, yet by great industry and economy[4] he was enabled to purchase his personal liberty.

At this time the remains of several Indian tribes, who originally possessed the right of soil, resided in Massachusetts; Cuffee became acquainted with a woman descended from one of those tribes, named Ruth Moses, and married her. He continued in habits of industry and frugality, and soon afterwards purchased a farm of 100 acres in Westport in Massachusetts.

Cuffee and Ruth had a family of ten children. The three eldest sons, David, Jonathan, and John are farmers in the neighbourhood of Westport, filling respectable situations in society, and endowed with good intellectual capacities. They are all married, and have families to whom they are giving good educations. Of six daughters four are respectably married, while two remain single.

Paul was born on the Island of Cutterhunkker, one of the Elizabeth Islands near New Bedford,[5] in the year 1759; when he was about 14 years of age his father died leaving a considerable property in land,

---

[1]*animating*: inspiring.
[2]*nidus*: Latin for "nest."
[3]*ult*: of last month.
[4]*industry and economy*: hard work and frugality.
[5]*New Bedford*: town in southeastern Massachusetts.

but which being at that time unproductive afforded but little provision for his numerous family, and thus the care of supporting his mother and sisters devolved upon his brothers and himself.

At this time Paul conceived that commerce furnished to industry more ample rewards than agriculture, and he was conscious that he possessed qualities which under proper culture[6] would enable him to pursue commercial employments with prospects of success; he therefore entered at the age of 16 as a common hand[7] on board of a vessel destined to the bay of Mexico, on a Whaling voyage. His second voyage was to the West Indies; but on his third he was captured by a British ship during the American war about the year 1776: after three months detention as a prisoner at New York, he was permitted to return home to Westport, where owing to the unfortunate continuance of hostilities he spent about 2 years in his agricultural pursuits. During this interval Paul and his brother John Cuffee were called on by the Collector[8] of the district, in which they resided, for the payment of a personal tax. It appeared to them, that, by the laws of the constitution of Massachusetts, taxation and the whole rights of citizenship were united. If the laws demanded of them the payment of personal taxes, the same laws must necessarily and constitutionally invest them with the rights of representing, and being represented, in the state Legislature. But they had never been considered as entitled to the privilege of voting at Elections, nor of being elected to places of trust and honor. Under these circumstances, they refused payment of the demands. The Collector resorted to the force of the laws, and after many delays and vexations, Paul and his brother deemed it most prudent to silence the suit by payment of the demands. But they resolved, if it were possible, to obtain the rights which they believed to be connected with taxation.

[6]*culture*: cultivation.
[7]*hand*: sailor.
[8]*Collector*: tax collector.

38

WILLIAM C. NELL

The Colored Patriots of the American Revolution
1855

William C. Nell was born in Boston in 1816 and died there in 1874. His book, The Colored Patriots of the American Revolution, *was the first book-length study of black participation in the Revolutionary War. It was also a political statement. Having dedicated his life to fighting racial injustice, Nell reasoned that if he could document the black contribution to the founding of the country, he could strengthen the case for the abolition of slavery. Here Nell recounts the wartime exploits of several African American Patriots, including Peter Salem (see Document 16) and James Forten of Philadelphia (1766–1842), who made a fortune after the war manufacturing sails for ships.*

[Samuel] Swett, in his "Sketches of Bunker Hill Battle," alludes to the presence of a colored man in that fight. He says:—"Major Pitcairn caused the first effusion of blood at Lexington. In that battle, his horse was shot under him, while he was separated from his troops. With presence of mind, he feigned himself slain; his pistols were taken from his holsters, and he was left for dead, when he seized the opportunity, and escaped. He appeared at Bunker Hill, and, says the historian, 'Among those who mounted the works was the gallant Major Pitcairn, who exultingly cried out, *"The day is ours!"* when a black soldier named [Peter] SALEM shot him through, and he fell. His agonized son received him in his arms, and tenderly bore him to the boats.' A contribution was made in the army for the colored soldier, and he was presented to Washington as having performed this feat."[1]

---

[1] In some engravings of the battle, this colored soldier occupies a prominent position; but in more recent editions, his figure is *non est inventus*. A significant, but inglorious omission. On some bills, however, of the Monumental Bank, Charlestown, and Freeman's Bank, Boston, his presence is manifest. [Nell's note]

From William C. Nell, *The Colored Patriots of the American Revolution* ... (Boston: Robert F. Wallcut, 1855), 21–23, 166–71.

Besides SALEM, there were quite a number of colored soldiers at Bunker Hill. Among them, TITUS COBURN, ALEXANDER AMES, and BARZILAI LEW, all of Andover; and also CATO HOWE, of Plymouth, — each of whom received a pension. Lew was a fifer. His daughter, Mrs. Dalton, now lives within a few rods[2] of the battle field.

SEYMOUR BURR was a slave in Connecticut, to a brother of Col. Aaron Burr, from whom he derived his name. Though treated with much favor by his master, his heart yearned for liberty, and he seized an occasion to induce several of his fellow slaves to escape in a boat, intending to join the British, that they might become freemen; but being pursued by their owners, armed with the implements of death, they were compelled to surrender.

Burr's master, contrary to his expectation, did not inflict corporeal punishment, but reminded him of the kindness with which he had been treated, and asked what inducement he could have for leaving him. Burr replied, *that he wanted his liberty.* His owner finally proposed, that if he would give him the bounty money,[3] he might join the American army, and at the end of the war be his own man. Burr, willing to make any sacrifice for his liberty, consented, and served faithfully during the campaign, attached to the Seventh Regiment, commanded by Colonel, afterwards Governor Brooks, of Medford. He was present at the siege of Fort Catskill, and endured much suffering from starvation and cold. After some skirmishing, the army was relieved by the arrival of Gen. Washington, who, as witnessed by him, shed tears of joy on finding them unexpectedly safe.

Burr married one of the Punkapog tribe of Indians, and settled in Canton, Mass. He received a pension from Government. His widow died in 1852, aged over one hundred years.

JEREMY JONAH served in the same Regiment, (Col. Brooks's,) at the same time with Seymour Burr. The two veterans used to make merry together in recounting their military adventures, especially the drill on one occasion, when Jonah stumbled over a stone heap; for which he was severely caned[4] by the Colonel. He drew a pension. . . .

JAMES FORTEN was born on the second day of September, 1766, and died on the Ides of March, 1842. He was the son of Thomas Forten, who died when James was but seven years old. His mother survived long after he had reached the years of maturity. In early life, he was

[2]*rods*: units of measurement equal to sixteen and a half feet.
[3]*bounty money*: enlistment bonus.
[4]*caned*: struck with a cane.

marked for great sprightliness and energy of character, a generous disposition, and indomitable courage, always frank, kind, courteous, and disinterested. In the year 1775, he left school, being then about nine years of age, having received a very limited education (and he never went to school afterwards) from that early, devoted, and worldwide known philanthropist, ANTHONY BENEZET. He was then employed at a grocery store and at home, when his mother, yielding to the earnest and unceasing solicitations of her son, whose young heart fired with the enthusiasm and feeling of the patriots and revolutionists of that day, with the firmness and devotion of a Roman matron, but with a heart *then* truly deemed American, gave the boy of her promise, the child of her heart and her hopes, to his country; upon the altar of its liberties she laid the apple of her eye, the jewel of her soul.

In 1780, then in his fourteenth year, he embarked on board the "*Royal Louis,*" Stephen Decatur, Senr., Commander, in the capacity of "powder-boy."[5] Scarce wafted[6] from his native shore, and perilled upon the dark blue sea, than he found himself amid the roar of cannon, the smoke of blood, the dying and the dead. Their ship was soon brought into action with an English vessel, the Lawrence, which, after a severe fight, in which great loss was sustained on both sides, and leaving every man wounded on board the "Louis" but himself, they succeeded in capturing, and brought her into port amid the loud huzzas and acclamations of the crowds that assembled upon the occasion. Forten, sharing largely in the feeling which so brilliant a victory had inspired, with fresh courage, and an unquenchable devotion to the interests of his native land, soon reëmbarked in the same vessel. In this cruise, however, they were unfortunate; for, falling in with three of the enemy's vessels,—the Amphyon, Nymph, and Pomona,—they were forced to strike their colors,[7] and become prisoners of war. It was at this juncture that his mind was harassed with the most painful forebodings, from a knowledge of the fact that rarely, if ever, were prisoners of his complexion exchanged; they were sent to the West Indies, and there doomed to a life of slavery. But his destiny, by a kind Providence, was otherwise. He was placed on board the Amphyon, Captain Beasly, who, struck with his open and honest countenance, made him the companion of his son. During one of those dull and monotonous periods which frequently occur on shipboard, young Beasly and Forten were engaged in a game at marbles,

---

[5]*powder-boy*: sailor on a warship responsible for bringing gunpowder to the cannon.
[6]*scarce wafted*: shortly after sailing away.
[7]*strike their colors*: lower their American flag.

when, with signal dexterity and skill, the marbles were upon every trial successively displaced by the unerring hand of Forten. This excited the surprise and admiration of his young companion, who, hastening to his father, called his attention to it. Upon being questioned as to the truth of the matter, and assuring the Captain that nothing was easier for him to accomplish, the marbles were again placed in the ring, and in rapid succession he redeemed his word.

A fresh and deeper interest was from that moment taken in his behalf. Captain Beasly proffered him a passage to England, tempted him with the allurements of wealth, under the patronage of his son, who was heir to a large estate there, the advantages of a good education, and freedom, equality and happiness, for ever. "No, NO!" was the invariable reply; "I am here a prisoner for the liberties of my country; *I never, NEVER, shall prove a traitor to her interests!*" What sentiment more exalted! What patriotism more lofty, devoted, and self-sacrificing! Indeed, with him, the feeling was, "America, with all thy faults, I love thee still"; for, with a full knowledge of the wrongs and outrages which she was then inflicting upon his brethren by the "ties of consanguinity[8] and of wrong," we see this persecuted and valiant son of hers, in the very darkest hour of his existence, when hope seemed to have departed from him, when the horrors of a hopeless West India slavery, with its whips for his shrinking flesh, and its chains for his freeborn soul, could only be dissipated by severing that tie, which, by the strongest cords of love, bound him to his native land, we see him standing up in the spirit of martyrdom, with a constancy of affection, and an invincibility of purpose, for the honor of his country, that place him above the noblest of the Caesars,[9] and entitle him to a monument towering above that which a Bonaparte erected at the *Place Vendôme.*

Beasly, having failed in inducing him to go to England, soon had him consigned to that floating and pestilential hell, the frigate "Old Jersey,"—giving him, however, as a token of his regard and friendship, a letter to the Commander of the prison-ship, highly commendatory of him, and also requesting that Forten should not be forgotten on the list of exchanges.[10] Thus (as he frequently remarked in after life) did a game of marbles save him from a life of West India servitude. In the mean while, his mother, at home, was in a state of mind bordering upon distraction, having learned that her son had been shot

---

[8]*consanguinity:* shared blood.
[9]*Caesars:* roman emperors.
[10]*exchanges:* prisoners to be exchanged.

from the foretop of the Royal Louis; but her mind was relieved, after he had been absent nearly eight months, by his appearing in person.

To return. While on board the "Old Jersey," amid the privations and horrors incident to that receiving ship of disease and death, no less than three thousand five hundred persons died; and, according to a statement of Edwards, eleven thousand in all perished, while she remained the receptacle of the American prisoners. . . . An officer of the American navy was about to be exchanged for a British prisoner, when the thoughtful mind of Forten conceived the idea of an easy escape for himself in the officer's chest; but, when about to avail himself of this opportunity, a fellow-prisoner, a youth, his junior in years, his companion and associate in suffering, was thought of. He immediately urged upon him to avail himself of the chances of an escape so easy. The offer was accepted, and Forten had the satisfaction of assisting in taking down the "chest of old clothes," as it was then called, from the side of the prison ship.

A Chronology of Black Americans in the Revolutionary Era

1763 Treaty of Paris ends Seven Years' War.

1765 Stamp Act and protest.

1766 North America's first Methodist church building is constructed in Frederick County, Maryland.

Quaker abolitionist Anthony Benezet publishes *A Caution and Warning to Great Britain and Her Colonies, in a Short Representation of the Calamitous State of the Enslaved Negroes in the British Dominions.*

1770 *September 30*: Death of George Whitefield, memorialized in a poem by Phillis Wheatley.

1770s Early in decade, the Reverend David George and his congregation form the first black Baptist church in the region that would become the United States, in Silver Bluff, South Carolina.

1772 Court of King's Bench's decision in the case of James Somerset is widely seen as abolishing slavery in England, Scotland, and Wales (but not the British colonies).

1773 Phillis Wheatley becomes the first African American to publish a book, *Poems on Various Subjects.*

1775 *April 19*: Battles of Lexington and Concord initiate the military phase of the Revolutionary War.

Summer: Slave revolts in South Carolina, Georgia, and North Carolina.

October 27: Battle of Hampton, Virginia. Enslaved Virginians play prominent roles.

November 14: Battle of Kemp's Landing, Virginia. Enslaved Virginians play prominent roles.

November 15 (dated November 7): Lord Dunmore, governor of Virginia, issues a proclamation promising freedom to any Patriot's slave who would fight for the king.

1776 *July 4*: Second Continental Congress adopts Declaration of Independence.

August: British troops land on Long Island and defeat the Continental Army.

December 25–26: Washington's army crosses the Delaware River and captures Hessian troops in Trenton, New Jersey.

1777 *September 11*: George Washington loses the Battle of Brandywine.

October 17: British general John Burgoyne surrenders his army to the Americans at Saratoga, New York.

1777–
1778 *Winter*: African Americans serve with both the Continental Army (headquartered at Valley Forge, Pennsylvania) and the British troops occupying Philadelphia.

1778 *February 6*: France enters the war on the American side.

December 29: Quamino Dolly plays a critical role in the British capture of Savannah, Georgia.

1779 *July 16*: Continental Army captures British fort at Stony Point, New York.

1780 *May 12*: British army captures Charleston, South Carolina, with the help of black soldiers and guides.

June: Pennsylvania legislature adopts a law saying that every Pennsylvanian born after its passage will be free.

1781 *October 19*: Lord Cornwallis, British southern commander, surrenders at Yorktown, Virginia, ensuring American victory in the Revolutionary War.

1783 *April*: Massachusetts Supreme Judicial Court abolishes slavery in the state (based on its interpretation of the bill of rights adopted with the state constitution three years earlier).

Summer: Guy Carleton, British commander in chief, decrees that Britain will keep its promise to free the slaves who fought in its armies. Most of the former slaves are transported to Nova Scotia.

September 3: Treaty of Paris ends American War of Independence.

1787 *July 13*: Congress bans slavery in the Northwest Territory (north of the Ohio River).

September 17: United States Constitution, endorsing slavery, is adopted and signed in Philadelphia.

1792 *January 15*: Fifteen ships of black Loyalists leave Nova Scotia headed for the British colony of Sierra Leone on the West African coast.

1793 Eli Whitney invents the cotton gin, which permits the profitable cultivation of short-staple cotton and the massive expansion of slavery.

1790s The African Methodist Episcopal (AME) Church and North America's first black Episcopal church are formed, both in Philadelphia.

1800 *October 10*: Gabriel is hanged for attempting to orchestrate a slave uprising in Richmond, Virginia.

Questions for Consideration

1. In what ways did the actions of African Americans help bring about the American Revolution?

2. If one of the Founding Fathers and one of his slaves were to write dictionary definitions of *freedom*, in what ways would the two definitions be similar and in what ways would they differ? Which definition is closest to your own?

3. Describe the many ways slaves in the Revolutionary era sought freedom. Which ways were most successful?

4. Find evidence for the great variety of skills that slaves possessed.

5. Identify and explain differences in the attitudes of Thomas Jefferson and Patrick Henry—two Founding Fathers who owned slaves—toward slavery and African Americans.

6. Identify and explain differences in the arguments that slaves and other opponents of slavery—at different times and in different places—used to try to convince other people to share their abhorrence of slavery.

7. Find evidence that opponents of slavery, including slaves, tried to use the rhetoric of the American Revolution to persuade white revolutionaries to oppose slavery.

8. Describe similarities and the differences in how northern and southern blacks experienced the Revolutionary War.

9. Why do you think conversion to Christianity was such an important theme for so many of the black writers in this volume? Do you find more evidence of variety or of consistency in these writers' religious experiences?

10. Assess the claim that slaves who escaped their owners during the Revolutionary War acquired more freedom than did any of the Founding Fathers.

11. How did various African Americans influence the outcome of the Revolutionary War?

12. How did white attitudes toward slavery change as a result of the American Revolution?

13. In what ways was the American Revolution good for African Americans? In what ways was it bad?

Selected Bibliography

INTERNET SITES

"Africans in America." www.pbs.org/wgbh/aia/home.html.
"The Atlantic Slave Trade and Slave Life in the Americas: A Visual Record."
   http://hitchcock.itc.virginia.edu/Slavery.
"Documenting the American South." http://docsouth.unc.edu/.
Nash, Gary B. "Thomas Peters: Millwright and Deliverer." http://revolution
   .h-net.msu.edu/essays/nash.html.

PRIMARY SOURCES

Allen, Richard. *The Life Experience and Gospel Labors of the Rt. Rev.
   Richard Allen.* Nashville, Tenn.: Abingdon Press, 1960.
Bruns, Roger, ed. *Am I Not a Man and a Brother: The Antislavery Crusade
   of Revolutionary America, 1688–1788.* New York: Chelsea House, 1977.
Carretta, Vincent, ed. *Unchained Voices: An Anthology of Black Authors in
   the English-Speaking World of the Eighteenth Century.* Lexington: Uni-
   versity Press of Kentucky, 2004.
Hodges, Graham Russell, ed. *The Black Loyalist Directory: African Ameri-
   cans in Exile after the American Revolution.* New York: Garland Press,
   1996.
Nell, William Cooper. *The Colored Patriots of the American Revolution.*
   New York: Arno Press, 1968 (orig. publ. 1855).
Taylor, Quintard, Jr., and Shirley Ann Wilson Moore, eds. *African
   American Women Confront the West, 1600–2000.* Norman: University of
   Oklahoma Press, 2003.
Wheatley, Phillis. *Complete Writings.* Ed. Vincent Carretta. New York:
   Penguin Books, 2001.
Windley, Lathan A. *Runaway Slave Advertisements: A Documentary His-
   tory from the 1730s to 1790.* Westport, Conn.: Greenwood Press, 1983.

SECONDARY SOURCES

Berlin, Ira. *Many Thousands Gone: The First Two Centuries of Slavery in
   North America.* Cambridge, Mass.: Harvard University Press, 1998.
Carretta, Vincent. *Equiano, the African: Biography of a Self-Made Man.*
   Athens: University of Georgia Press, 2005.

Davis, David Brion. *The Problem of Slavery in an Age of Revolution*. Ithaca, N.Y.: Cornell University Press, 1975.

Dusinberre, William. *Them Dark Days: Slavery in the American Rice Swamps*. New York: Oxford University Press, 1996.

Egerton, Douglas R. *Gabriel's Rebellion: The Virginia Slave Conspiracies of 1800 and 1802*. Chapel Hill: University of North Carolina Press, 1993.

———. *Death or Liberty: African Americans and Revolutionary America*. New York: Oxford University Press, 2009.

Fenn, Elizabeth. *Pox Americana: The Great Smallpox Epidemic of 1775–82*. New York: Hill and Wang, 2001.

Finkelman, Paul. *Slavery and the Founders: Race and Liberty in the Age of Jefferson*. Armonk, N.Y.: M. E. Sharpe, 1996.

Frey, Sylvia R. *Water from the Rock: Black Resistance in a Revolutionary Age*. Princeton, N.J.: Princeton University Press, 1991.

Goldstone, Lawrence. *Dark Bargain: Slavery, Profits, and the Struggle for the Constitution*. New York: Walker and Company, 2005.

Gordon-Reed, Annette. *Thomas Jefferson and Sally Hemings: An American Controversy*. Charlottesville: University Press of Virginia, 1997.

Holton, Woody. *Forced Founders: Indians, Debtors, Slaves, and the Making of the American Revolution in Virginia*. Chapel Hill: University of North Carolina Press, 1999.

Kaplan, Sidney, and Emma Nogrady Kaplan. *The Black Presence in the Era of the American Revolution*, rev. ed. Amherst: University of Massachusetts Press, 1989.

Kulikoff, Allan. *Tobacco and Slaves: The Development of Southern Cultures in the Chesapeake, 1680–1800*. Chapel Hill: University of North Carolina Press, 1986.

Lepore, Jill. *New York Burning: Liberty, Slavery, and Conspiracy in Eighteenth-Century Manhattan*. New York: Alfred A. Knopf, 2005.

Levy, Andrew. *The First Emancipator: The Forgotten Story of Robert Carter, the Founding Father Who Freed His Slaves*. New York: Random House, 2005.

Linebaugh, Peter, and Marcus Rediker. *The Many-Headed Hydra: Sailors, Slaves, Commoners, and the Hidden History of the Revolutionary Atlantic*. Boston: Beacon Press, 2000.

McDonnell, Michael A. *The Politics of War: Race, Class, and Conflict in Revolutionary Virginia*. Chapel Hill: University of North Carolina Press, 2007.

Morgan, Edmund S. *American Slavery, American Freedom: The Ordeal of Colonial Virginia*. New York: Norton, 1975.

Morgan, Philip. *Slave Counterpoint: Black Culture in the Eighteenth Century Chesapeake and Low Country*. Chapel Hill: University of North Carolina Press, 1998.

Nash, Gary B. *Forging Freedom: The Formation of Philadelphia's Black Community, 1720–1840*. Cambridge, Mass.: Harvard University Press, 1988.

————. *The Forgotten Fifth: African Americans in the Age of Revolution.* Cambridge, Mass.: Harvard University Press, 2006.

————. *The Unknown American Revolution: The Unruly Birth of Democracy and the Struggle to Create America.* New York: Penguin, 2005.

Olwell, Robert. *Masters, Slaves and Subjects: The Culture of Power in the South Carolina Low Country, 1740–1790.* Ithaca, N.Y.: Cornell University Press, 1998.

O'Shaughnessy, Andrew Jackson. *An Empire Divided: The American Revolution and the British Caribbean.* Philadelphia: University of Pennsylvania Press, 2000.

Pulis, John W., ed. *Moving On: Black Loyalists in the Afro-Atlantic World.* New York: Garland, 1999.

Pybus, Cassandra. *Epic Journeys of Freedom: Runaway Slaves of the American Revolution and Their Global Quest for Liberty.* Boston: Beacon Press, 2006.

Quarles, Benjamin. *The Negro in the American Revolution.* Chapel Hill: University of North Carolina Press, 1961.

Schama, Simon. *Rough Crossings: Britain, the Slaves and the American Revolution.* London: BBC Books, 2005.

Sensbach, Jon F. *Rebecca's Revival: Creating Black Christianity in the Atlantic World.* Cambridge, Mass.: Harvard University Press, 2005.

————. *A Separate Canaan: The Making of an Afro-Moravian World in North Carolina, 1763–1840.* Chapel Hill: University of North Carolina Press, 1998.

Sidbury, James. *Ploughshares into Swords: Race, Rebellion, and Identity in Gabriel's Virginia, 1730–1810.* Cambridge: Cambridge University Press, 1997.

Taylor, Quintard, Jr. *In Search of the Racial Frontier: African Americans in the American West, 1528–1990.* New York: Norton, 1998.

Thornton, John. *Africa and Africans in the Making of the Atlantic World, 1400–1680.* Athens: University of Georgia Press, 1991.

Waldstreicher, David. *Runaway America: Benjamin Franklin, Slavery, and American Revolution.* New York: Hill and Wang, 2004.

Wiencek, Henry. *An Imperfect God: George Washington, His Slaves, and the Creation of America.* New York: Farrar, Straus and Giroux, 2003.

Wilson, Ellen Gibson. *The Loyal Blacks.* New York: Capricorn Books, 1976.

Wood, Peter H. *Black Majority: Negroes in Colonial South Carolina from 1670 through the Stono Rebellion.* New York: Norton, 1974.

————. *Strange New Land: Africans in Colonial America, 1526–1776.* New York: Oxford University Press, 2003.

Index

149